# TALKING DIRTY

A Bawdy Compendium of Colorful Language,
Humorous Insults & Wicked Jokes

Carroll & Graf Publishers, Inc.
New York

Copyright © 1993 by Reinhold Aman

Published by arrangement with Robson Books Ltd., London

First Carroll & Graf edition 1994

Carroll & Graf Publishers, Inc.
260 Fifth Avenue
New York, NY 10001

Library of Congress Cataloging-in-Publication Data

```
Talking dirty : a bawdy compendium of colorful language, humorous
  insults & wicked jokes / [edited by Reinhold Aman]. -- 1st Carroll &
  Graf ed.
      p.   cm.
   ISBN 0-7867-0164-1 : $11.95 ($16.95 Can.)
   1. American wit and humor.  2. English language--Obscene words-
 -Humor.   3. Blessing and cursing--Humor.   4. Invective--Humor.
 5. Sex--Humor.   I. Aman, Reinhold.
 PN6162.T27  1994
 818'.540208--dc20                                      94-19640
                                                           CIP
```

Manufactured in the United States of America

# CONTENTS

# INTRODUCTION

Every day around the world, tens of thousands of people are humiliated, fired, fined, jailed, injured, killed, or driven to suicide because of *maledicta*: insults, slurs, curses, threats, blasphemies, vulgarities, obscenities, and other offensive words and expressions. *Maledicta* ('bad words' in Latin) cover a broad spectrum of language traditionally avoided in public by prudish professors, prim word-popes, and other properlings who none the less use many such words in private. The opposite of prayer and praise, *maledicta* are the black sheep of language that most people use but few talk or write about.

Nasty language is heard most often in stressful, angry and other emotionally charged situations. It ranges from mild terms such as 'She's no spring chicken' (meaning: she's old) to the vilest language. It is spoken as fluently in universities, clubhouses, and elegant corporate offices, as it is in the gutter. 'Bad words' are used by princes and peasants, by priests and prostitutes.

There are many types of verbal aggression, ranging from one-word slurs ('dickhead') and earthy comparisons ('He's as horny as a three-peckered billy goat') to sneaky insults understood only by the in-group: calling a Hindi speaker *sālā* (literally, 'brother-in-law') actually is an insult; it means, 'I slept with your sister; your sister is a slut.'

This anthology, selected from the 3,200 pages of *Maledicta: The International Journal of Verbal Aggression*, presents a smörgåsbord of serious and light-hearted contributions from English and other tongues. They embrace many fields of study and shed much light on human nature, on moral value systems, and on the psychological, linguistic, and sociological aspects of language.

'Bad words' have existed ever since the first humans broke their spears or were attacked by hostile tribes. We know only a minute fraction of former and current *maledicta* because there were no written records until some 5,000 years ago and because most linguists and lexicographers refuse to study or record such negative language out of fear of staining their professional image. Thus, in 1965, I decided to dedicate my life to the collection and analysis of all those words and expressions shunned by cacademia and to publish the results in our irregular journal *Maledicta*, with the motto: 'They say it – we print it.'

Many properlings look down on the few brave men and women who study 'dirty' and nasty words. Strange as it may sound, to prudish folks the *word* is more repulsive than the *thing* for which it stands. A urologist examining a diseased penis is an honoured chap, but a philologist collecting synonyms for 'penis' is a dirty old man.

In the past twenty-eight years I have gathered material from more than 220 languages, from today's slang and ethnic 'jokes' to 5,000-year-old book-thief curses. And yet, we have only scratched the surface. Almost weekly new contributions arrive in my office, from New Guinean Pidgin-English glossaries and American pizza-shop slang to Finnish euphemisms and Tibetan monks' requests such as *'âbu dânna?* ('Will you sodomize me?') Unfortunately, I have not yet received any insult glossaries in Welsh or Gaelic, or studies of abusive language from Jamaica, South Africa, East India, and New Zealand. I have been unable to gather derogatory sayings from Yorkshire to Suffolk, and slang from Oxford students or London taxi-drivers. Contributions are always welcome.

It may sound blasphemous, but the Bible contains almost as much verbal aggression and as many Godly curses and 'dirty' topics as *Talking Dirty*, so please don't be too hasty to condemn this book. It provides a good-natured look at bad-tempered people the world over and should make you chuckle and think. Perhaps this book will make you more tolerant of others by realizing your own deviations from somebody else's norms.

Enjoying this work won't turn you into a mean-mouthed mule-driver. When you are frustrated or angry, there is nothing more therapeutic than tears – or a blue-streaked verbal blast. Any civilized person will agree that verbal bullets are better than metal bullets. And the tongue is always mightier than the sword, in this or any *annus horribilis*.

Dr Reinhold Aman
Editor, *Maledicta*
P.O. Box 14123
Santa Rosa, CA 95402–6123,
USA

# ODE TO THOSE FOUR-LETTER WORDS

(Anon)

*Banish the use of those four-letter words*
*Whose meanings are never obscure.*
*The Angles and Saxons, those bawdy old birds,*
*Were vulgar, obscene, and impure.*
*But cherish the use of the weak-kneed phrase*
*That never quite says what you mean;*
*Far better you stick to your hypocrite ways*
*Than be vulgar, or coarse, or obscene.*

When *Nature is calling*, plain speaking is out,
When ladies, God bless 'em, are milling about,
You *make water, wee-wee*, or *empty the glass*;
You can *powder your nose*; *'Excuse me'* may pass;
*Shake the dew off the lily*; *see a man 'bout a dog*;
Or when everyone's *soused*, it's *condensing the fog*,
But be pleased to consider and remember just this –
That only in Shakespeare do characters **piss**!

You may speak of a *movement*, or *sit on a seat*,
*Have a passage*, or *stool*, or simply *excrete*;
Or say to the others, *'I'm going out back,'*
Then groan in pure joy in that smelly old shack.
You can go *lay a cable*, or *do number two*,
Or *sit on the toidy* and *make a do-do*,
But ladies and men who are socially fit
Under no provocation will go take a **shit**!

When your dinners are hearty with onions and beans,
With garlic and claret and bacon and greens;
Your bowels get so busy distilling a *gas*
That Nature insists you permit it to *pass*.

You are very polite, and you try to *exhale*
Without noise or odour – you frequently fail –
Expecting a zephyr, you carefully start,
But even a deaf one would call it a **fart!**

A woman has *bosoms*, a *bust* or a *breast*.
Those *lily-white swellings* that bulge 'neath her vest;
They are *towers of ivory*, *sheaves of new wheat*;
In a moment of passion, ripe *apples* to eat.
You may speak of her *nipples* as small *rings of fire*
With hardly a question of raising her ire;
But by Rabelais's beard, she'll throw fifteen fits
If you speak of them roundly as good honest **tits!**

It's a *cavern of joy* you are thinking of now,
A warm, tender *field* just awaiting the plough
It's a quivering *pigeon* caressing your hand,
Or that sweet little *pussy* that makes a man stand.
Or perhaps it's a *flower*, a *grotto*, a *well*,
The *hope of the world*, or a *velvety hell*.
But, friend, heed this warning, beware the affront
Of aping a Saxon: don't call it a **cunt!**

Though a lady repel your advance, she'll be kind
Just as long as you intimate what's on your mind.
You may tell her you're *hungry*, you *need to be swung*,
You may ask her *to see how your etchings are hung*.
You may mention the *ashes that need to be hauled*;
*Put the lid on her sauce-pan*, but don't be too bold;
For the moment you're forthright, get ready to duck –
The girl isn't born yet who'll stand for 'Let's **fuck!**'

*Banish the use of those four-letter words*
*Whose meanings are never obscure.*
*The Angles and Saxons, those bawdy old birds,*
*Were vulgar, obscene, and impure.*
*But cherish the use of the weak-kneed phrase*
*That never quite says what you mean:*
*Far better you stick to your hypocrite ways,*
*Than be vulgar, or coarse, or obscene.*

# TERMS OF ABUSE, TERMS OF ENDEARMENT, AND PET NAMES FOR BREASTS AND OTHER NAUGHTY BODY PARTS

(Reinhold Aman)

This article deals with terms of abuse and endearment. They are divided into various groups: in *general* and *descriptive* ones which, in the case of penis, show the designations for all kinds of such organs — whether they be big or small, thick or thin, long or short, soft or hard, straight or bent, wrinkled or smooth, and whatever else penes look like and give them names to characterize their appearance and functions. As to female breasts, the descriptive terms are designations for every conceivable type: big and small, hard and soft, pendulous, leathery, asymmetrical, and more. There are far too many terms to be included in this article; they will be presented later and, ultimately, in my DRAT, the *Dictionary of Regional Anatomical Terms*.

Another two groups are presented, covering *endearing* and *abusive* terms for sexual body parts, as well as *pet names* for bawdy body parts used by individuals and their spouses or friends.

Rather than boring you with too many statistics and tables, I will present some general comments on the findings and list the most commonly-cited endearing and offensive names, with a few remarks about my informants.

The *sex* of the informants was the only significant factor as to whether they considered certain body-part terms 'nice' or 'nasty'. The other characteristics did not, neither *age*, which ranges from 14 to 76 years, nor *race*, whether white, black, American Indian, Hispanic, Asian or mixed. *Religion* also

1

shows no influence, ranging from Orthodox Jews and Roman Catholics to Greek Orthodox and Atheists. Finally, the *geographic background* of informants shows little difference in nice and nasty terms, whether they are from the United States, Canada, Great Britain, South Africa, Australia, or New Zealand.

So that you get an idea of who my helpful informants are, a few numbers are necessary: as to *sex*, of the 318 total replies 86 are female and 232 are male; or, more specifically, 196 are heterosexual males, 22 homosexual males, and 14 bisexual males, as well as 78 heterosexual females, 2 lesbians, and 6 bisexual females. As to *race*, 308 are white, 8 are black, and 2 are of mixed background. By *religion*, 84 are Catholic, 35 Jewish, 35 Methodist, 108 practise no religion, and the remaining 56 are of various persuasions.

# TERMS OF ENDEARMENT AND ABUSE

## Breasts: 'Nice' Terms

Regarding *terms of endearment and abuse for women's breasts*, of the 318 informants 291 provided nice terms, while 29 did not; 251 provided nasty terms, but 67 use no nasty terms. The most common nice terms for breasts are, by decreasing frequency: **breasts** (110, or about one-third of the respondents), **tits** (73), **boobs** (65), **titties** (30), and **boobies** (13). Other multiple entries are **bosom** or **bosoms** (8), **knockers** (8), **jugs** (6), 4 each **chest** and **melons**, **tomatoes** (3), and 2 each **bazooms**, **bust**, **globes**, **hooters**, **mammaries**, and **teats**.

The remaining nice terms were single occurrences, sometimes given with preceding adjectives: **beautiful chest, beautiful pair, blossoms, boobulars, borstjes** (Dutch, 'breasts'), **bubbies, bumpers, cantaloupes, chichis** (Spanish, 'tits'), **chichitas** (Spanish, 'titties'), **cycuszki** (Polish, diminutive of **cycki**, cf. German *Zitze*, 'teat'), **dairy farm, diddies, dugs, figure, frontage, groodies, head-lights, juicy peaches, love-pillows, mazoomas, mounds, mountains, Möppchen** (German, diminutive, unknown meaning), **nay-nays, nice handful, nice puppies, nice set, norks, pair, peaches, pechitos** (Spanish, 'breasties'), **pretty lungs, porcelain spheres** (reported by a bisexual male), **rising beauties, set of jugs, soft cadaby** (unknown meaning), **sweat-glands, sweetest valley, tetinas** and **tetitas** (Spanish, 'titties'), **the girls, tsitskelakh** (Yiddish, 'titties'), and **the warmest valley.**

## Breasts: 'Nasty' Terms

While *tits* was commonly cited as a nice term (73 times), it was also considered a nasty term for breasts, 116 times, sometimes even by the same informants. Many qualified their responses in such cases by saying that it depends on the context, that is, who uses the term *tits* under what circumstances, with what tone of voice, facial expression, and the like. Also, they noted that the nice or nasty connotation is established by the preceding adjective. For example, in 'You have great tits' or 'What a lovely pair of tits!' the word is positive, nice, whereas in 'ugly tits' or 'Look at her sagging tits', the word *tits* has negative connotations. Still, in absolute terms, *tits* is considered by almost twice as many people nasty rather than nice.

Negatively-valued or nasty terms for breasts, in order of frequency, are: **tits** (116), **jugs** (23), **dugs** (20), **boobs** (18), **knockers** (13), **udders** (9), **bags** (7), 4 each **cans** and **melons**, 3 each **cow-tits, mosquito-bites, sagging tits,** and **titties.** Two responses each: **balloons, breasts, fried eggs, fuckin' tits, knobs, pancakes** and **saggy tits.**

The following nasty terms were reported once each. In several cases, I have included the adjectives that were given with the nouns: 'anything besides *breasts*', **bazooms, beaver-tails, bellys, body, boulders, chest, draggy udders, dried-up titties, droopers, dzwony** (Polish, 'bells'), **Euter** (German, 'udder'), **fat ugly wrinkled bottles, fat-sacks, fatty breasts, flab hangings, flabby melons, flapjacks, floppers, floppy tits, floppy whites, flops, globes, hairy stubs, hanging tits, Hänger** (German, 'hangers', 'hanging ones'), **honkers, lumps, lung-nuts, massive mammaries, milkers, milk-buckets, milk-glands, milk-sacks, molehills, no tits, old saggy tits, paps, peanuts,**

pimientos fritos (Spanish, 'fried green peppers'), **pimples,
pimples on chest, pus glands, rocks, sagging summer squash,
saggy pig tits, scar-crossed prunes, shit-bags, skin, slugs,
sweater-meat, teats, tieten** (Dutch, 'teats'), **tired old tits, tube-
socks with a golfball, ugly fat knockers, ugly jugs, waterbags**
and **wrinkled tits.**

*Bosoms* is used quite often, even though this plural is wrong,
because *bosom* means both breasts. A woman can't have
*bosoms*, unless she has a second set of breasts (preferably on
her back, for dancing). The only woman I can think of who
had *bosoms* was the Graeco-Roman goddess Artemis or Diana
of Ephesus who, as shown on a statue, sported at least 19
breasts – the ideal patron saint of the typical American
mammophile.

Comparing *boobs* with *tits*, 65 informants think *boobs* is a
nice term, while 18 think it is a nasty one. This 3:1 ratio shows
that *boobs* is considered by most people to be a nice term. In
the case of *tits*, and remembering the earlier comments about
context, 73 respondents consider it a nice term, whereas 116
think it is a nasty word. As to the gender of informants, 14
females say that *boobs* is a nice term, but 10 think it is nasty.
Eleven females think *tits* is a nice term, but twice as many, 22,
consider it nasty. Eight homosexual and bisexual men think
*boobs* is nice, while 2 say it is nasty. Seven gay males say that
*tits* is nice, and 10 think it is nasty. As to lesbian and bisexual
females, 2 think *boobs* is nice, but not one thinks it is nasty.
Two of them say *tits* is nice, but 5 consider it nasty.

## Penis: 'Nice' Terms

Of our informants, 252 provided nice terms for penis, 66 did
not. The most frequently-cited nice name is **cock** (86), followed
by **dick** (37), 17 each **pecker** and **penis**, **prick** (15), 8 each
**love-muscle** and **peter**, **rod** (5), 4 each **pee-pee**, **sausage**, **tool,
wang, weenie** and **willy**, 3 each **dong, meat** and **shlong** (Yiddish, 'snake'), 2 each **dickie, dink, goober, little friend,
love-stick, manhood, member, thing** and **wanger.**

All others are cited only once: **baldheaded candidate, bat,** best friend, big one, big piece of meat, big wand, cock of death, dinghy, dog, doohicky, dork, ducky-bird, dyduś (Polish, no lit. meaning), fat peter, friend, hacker, hampton, hampton wick, hard-on, horse's cock, hunky, jelly-bean, John Thomas, John Willie, johnson (a black term, named after a large American railway brake lever), joint, jolly roger, jongeheer (Dutch, 'young fellow'), joystick, knob, lingam (Sanskrit, from the *Kamasutra*), little man, lollipop, love machine, love-gun, love-wand, maly (Polish, 'little one'), member virile, muscle, nob, oak tree, one-eyed trouser-trout, organ, parts, penie, pet snake, pichita de oro (Spanish, 'golden cock'), Piephahn (German children's language, 'dicky-bird', lit. 'peeping cock'), pink torpedo, pitonguita (Spanish, 'little python'), privates, pud, puss, pussy, rig, Schniedelwutz (German, unknown meaning, but dialectal *Wutz* means 'pig' and 'rolled object'), Schniepel (German children's language, lit. 'tip, point'), schwanger (unknown meaning; perhaps from German, 'pregnant'), shmok (Yiddish, lit. probably 'snake'), silky appendage, snatch pointer, soft, steel-rod, sugar-stick, third leg, throbbing member, throbbing muscle of pure love, tool of pleasure, trout, unit, wiener and yang fella.

## Penis: 'Nasty' Terms

Now we come to nasty names for the penis. Of the 318 total, 246 informants provided nasty terms, but 72 had none. As can be expected, about a dozen of the nasty terms for penis also show up in the nice column. Here are the nasty terms, again by decreasing frequency of citation: prick (81), cock (54), dick (21), shlong (8), pecker (6), 5 each needle-dick, dong and dork, and 3 times each pencil-dick, penis, salami, shmok and wee-wee. There were 2 mentions each of fuck-stick, thing, tool, weenie and worm.

The following terms appear once each as nasty terms for the penis, several times prefixed with *little*: big clit, bitte (French, 'dick'), blood-breaker, bug-fucker, capullito (Spanish, 'little [plant] bud'), chuj (Russian and Polish, 'prick'), cod, colostomy, crank, cunt-stabber, dangle-dong, dead worm, dimple-dick, dink, dipstick, dog, dribble-cock, dust cover for cunt, flaccid prick, fuckpole, God's revenge on a woman (submitted by a female), gourd, green-coloured dick, half a cob, joy-stick, lifeless, limp-dick, limp-prick, little dick, little peter, little pinkie, little sliver of flesh, little stick, little wiener, little worm, lul (Dutch, 'prick'), man-meat, middle leg, millimetre-peter, minus a pinus, nothin' cock, old goat-peter, old warty cod, organ, pee-wee, penal dick, pichicorta (Spanish, 'short dick'), piddler, pimple, pimple-prick, pine, piss-pipe, pisser, pissworm, poker, pots (Yiddish), puny prick, pus-rod, rod, rotten meat, scorz (unknown meaning), scrawny piece, shaft, shmendrik (Yiddish, 'little nobody, nincompoop'), shorty, shriveller, shvants, (Yiddish, 'tail'), small, stupid dink, syphilitic prick, teeny, tossergash, ugly little dog-dick, unit, useless, verga (Spanish, 'dick'), wet noodle, wet spaghetti, wimpy dick and wrinkled dick.

## Vulva: 'Nice' Terms

In this section I'll present names for vulva and vagina considered nice. Many informants, as also the general population, do not distinguish between *vulva* (the outer parts) and *vagina* (the channel, sheath).

As in the case of penis, many terms for vulva considered nasty also appear as nice terms in this collection. Of the 318 informants, 234 provided nice terms for vulva, while 84 had no nice name for it. Those who did not provide a nice name were of all sexual persuasions, by the way. Nasty terms were provided by 274 respondents, but 44 had no negative terms. By frequency, here is a list of nice names for vulva and vagina: the most frequent name was **pussy** (125), followed by **cunt** (20 times, including by 4 females), 9 each **snatch** and **vagina**, **twat** (8), **honey-pot** (6), 5 times each **beaver** and **muff**, 4 times each **love-tunnel** and **puss**, 3 times each **cunny**, **fanny**, **hole**, **love-box** and **quim**, and twice each **cooze**, **furburger**, **love-nest** and **rosebud**.

Other nice names mentioned once are: **baby-factory**, **belle chose** (French, 'beautiful thing'), **box**, **bush**, **centricpart**, chochito (Spanish, 'pussy'), conchita (Spanish, 'little shell') dessert, Döschen (German, 'little box'), fascinating furpiece, fount of femininity, fun-zone, fur-pie, fuzzy-muzzy, garden of love, Gizelle (name), hairy Mary, Holiday Inn, honeydew, inner self, inside, jelly-roll, joy-furrow, kitty, kitty-kat, kuciapka (Polish, no literal meaning), li'l pussy, lips, little kitten, love-cleft, love-organ, love-sheath, lovely flower, lunch, mick, Muschi (German, 'kitty-cat' and woman's name), nookie, parts, peach-fish, play-pen, pocket, poo-poo, poontang, poozle, pud, slit, snackbar, sneetje (Dutch, 'little slit'), soft furry mound of love, spread, sweet cunt, sweet pussy, tee-tee, thing, tight snatch, treasure-box, tunnel of love, vag, vertical smile, warm place, wazoo, wily and yoni (Sanskrit, from the *Kama Sutra*).

## Vulva: 'Nasty' Terms

In his *1811 Dictionary of the Vulgar Tongue*, Captain Grose wrote that C**t is 'a nasty name for a nasty thing'. The most commonly-cited nasty word for the female organ of lust is still cunt, 179 times out of 318 responses, plus 14 instances where it is preceded by a specific adjective. Next in frequency is gash (20), hole (17), twat (14), pussy (13), 9 each slit and snatch, 3 each canyon, smelly cunt and stinkhole, 2 each box, crack, dirty cunt, fish and stinky cunt.

The remaining terms appear once each: 'anything related to fish or smell', ass, bayonet wound, bearded clam, beaver-trap, big cunt, big cave, cheese factory, chocho gordo (Spanish, 'fat cunt'), clit, cow-cunt, crater, dirty hole, empty tunnel, envy-city, face, fanny, fat rabbit, fish-box, flabby cunt, foul-smelling cunt, fuck-hole, greedy pussy-lips, kut (Dutch, 'cunt'), man-eater, man-entrapment, man-trap, Möse (German, 'twat'), open well, open wound, panocha (Spanish, lit. 'coarse brown sugar'), pee-hole, pestosa (Spanish, 'diseased, stinky one'), piss-flaps, pizda (Polish, 'cunt'), podrida (Spanish, 'rotten, putrid one'), pox-ridden cunt, prat, rat-hole, rotten crotch, sardine can, scabby cunt, Schlabberfotze (German, 'slobbery, watery cunt'), scum-twat, scumbag, siffed-up cunt-hole (from *syphilis*), slash, slime-hole, slippery slut, sloppy bot, smell-hole, smelly pussy, snapper, something crawled in and died, sperm-canal, split-tail, stink-pit, tuna, vag, vagina, Votze (German, 'cunt'; also spelled Fotze), wet-mop, wound, wrinkled cunt and yeast-mill.

## GENITAL PET NAMES

After this litany of nasties, I'll present some comments on pet names for sexual organs. There were fewer than expected actual pet names, which was a surprise. Even many homosexuals, many of whom appear to be very much in touch with their genitals, as it were, have fewer pet names than expected. One should think that now as we are entering the Golden Age of Masturbation – no thanks to AIDS – people would be paying more attention to their only truly safe sex partner and have more appealing names than 'my thing' or 'the old fella'.

There are also jokes about penis pet names. Ingrid B. told me a German joke about what European women call a penis: German women call it 'Curtain' (comes down after every act); English women call it 'Gentleman' (rises in front of a lady); French women name it 'Chanson' (goes from mouth to mouth). Russian women call it 'Guerrilla' (you never know if it's coming from the front or the rear).

Most surprising was the number of people who not only have pet names for their own and their friends' sexual organs, but also for other body parts and related equipment. For example, one woman calls her left breast 'Alice' and her right breast 'Phyllis'. Another woman names her breasts 'Judo' and 'Jello'. An 18-year-old calls hers 'Tasty' and 'Delicious'. Several years ago, when I was introduced to the wife of a New York friend and sex researcher, I was tempted to ask her whether she calls her breasts 'Schleswig' and 'Holstein,' respectively, as her ancestors came from the German state called Schleswig-Holstein. Considering the importance of breasts in many cultures, mammaries ought to produce playful mammonyms, such as *Tutti Frutti*, *Lo & Behold*, or *Sweet & Low*.

Two males have pet names for their **hands:** one calls his right hand 'Rosy Palm', after the well-known 'Rosy Palm and her five daughters', and another calls it 'Little Jo-Jo', after his girlfriend's name. One lady wrote me that she calls her right hand 'Little Reinhold'.

**Testicles** also have pet names. One professor of biology calls his testes 'John Henry'. Bill A.'s 24-year-old wife calls his penis 'Little Buddy' and his testicles 'Little Buddy's buddies'.

Interestingly, **vibrators** also have pet names. One of our New York informants calls her vibrator 'Charlie', and a Wisconsin musician calls her 'B-flat', after the sound it emits at low speed. She also has a second pet name for it, the German 'Wunderorgasmusmaschine'.

To stimulate readers into pet-naming their privates, I suggest *Sumer* (it's *icumen in*), or *My Prince* (someday he'll come) or *The South* (it will rise again), as well as *Trouble* (many men like to get into it).

## Penis Pet Names

Of the 204 pet names for penis collected so far, 117 are used by heterosexual men for their own organ, and 49 by their wives or girlfriends. Pet names used by homosexuals are discussed later.

Many of the penis pet names used by males are common terms, such as **dick** (15), **cock,** (13), **pecker** (6), **prick** (5), **willie** (4), and twice **boy,** but there are very specific ones, of which the cleverest is by an Ohio physician who calls his penis 'His Royal Highness, Prince Everhard of the Netherlands'. Other pet names are often prefixed with *my* or *my little*. Here is the list of penis pet names gathered so far: **ace** (as in 'ace in the hole'), **ascent, baby's arm, banger, big fella, big log, blue-steel, boy** (as in 'You hungry, boy?'), **chachiporra** (Spanish, 'big stick'), **Charlie, chinchin** (Japanese children's language), **o-chinchin** (the same, with the honorific prefix o-), **crank, dong, Elmer, Pudd, flip** (from Philip), **Fred, friend, godgiven groover, Harvey** (after the giant rabbit in the movie), **husky, il mio amico** (Italian, 'my friend'), **it, John, John Henry Longfellow**

(*John* and *Henry* are pet names for his testicles), **John Thomas,
joy-stick, junior, knob, leather cigar, little boy blue** (as in 'come
blow my horn'), **little buddy, little dickie, little guy with the
German helmet** (from *German helmet*, a term for glans), **little
guy, little John, love-muscle, love pump, love sceptre, ma bitte**
(French, 'my dick'), **mack, mate, Milton, Mr Happy, Mr
Johnson, Mr Penis, my friend, my little friend, my thang, oak
tree, old baldy, Opie, oral tube** (as in 'Talk to me through this
tube'), **Oscar, Ozymandias** ('. . . and despair,' from Shelley's
sonnet), **Pedro, pee-dee, pee-pee, penis, Percy, Pete, Peter,
Pogo, purple throbber, rhythm and blues, rod, Roger, Roscoe**
(twice), **Rufus, Schniepel** (German, 'dicky,' lit. 'point tip'),
**simba, spunky, tally-whacker, tarzoon, teenager, the ever-
famous, thing, Thomas Jefferson** (as in 'all men are created
equal'), **Throckmorton, tiddelly pod, Tom, tool of pleasure,
toy, unit, Vivitar** (after the enlarging camera lens), **Walter,
wang, war-head, weapon, wee-wee, Wicked Willie, Winston**
(as in 'tastes good, like a cigarette should') and **Yogi** (after the
cartoon character).

Women use pet names for the penis of their husbands or
male friends, too, sometimes the same names as their male
partners use. **Dick** was most frequent, with 4 listings, followed
by 2 each **cock, Fred, him, John Thomas, little friend, tool,
weenie** and **whang.** The remaining occur once each: **ace, bat,
big hard hot throbbing dick, cutums, deck, Freddie** (after
her husband), **goober, good buddy, himself, his highness,
junior, little dickie, little Elvis, little one, lollipop, Lou**
(husband's name), **love-wand, Matthew** (husband's name),
**moby** (from *Moby Dick*), **mouse, Mr Happy, Mr Microphone** (as in 'I'll be back to pick it up'), **Mr Wang, my fella,
my friend, panchito** (Spanish, 'little belly' and man's name),
**pecker-mine, pee-pee, peeper, Pete, rod, Russell the love mus-
cle, sausage & eggs** (for penis and testes), **special friend,
super-dong, tally-whacker, the indicator, toy, Walter, Willie,
Willy, winger** and **woofer.**

## Vulva and Vagina Pet Names

Out of the 86 women, 34 have pet names for their own vulva, and 101 males use pet names for their wives' or female friends' genitals.

The women's most frequent pet name is **pussy** (13), but terms considered nasty by others also appear in this listing, often preceded by *my*: twice each **box, pussy** and **vulva**, and once each **coochy, cunny, cunt, friend, furry bits, good pussy, herself, hot wet pussy, junioress, Little Debbie, little kitty, Matthilda, mouse's hole, my burger, peach-fish, precious pudenda, Priscilla, pussy galore, pussy, sex, snatch, tesorito** (Spanish, 'little treasure'), **Virginia** and **womanhood**.

The most frequent pet name for vulva by males also is **pussy** (41 times), followed by **cunt** (7), **vagina** (4), **twat** (3), and 2 each **bush, honey-pot, lips, muffy, peach-fish, rose-bud, snatch** and **sweet cunt**. Other pet names mentioned are: **belle chose** (French, 'beautiful thing'), **box, buggy, cave, chatte** (French, 'cat'), **chochito mío** (Spanish, 'my little pussy'), **cock, coño** (Spanish, 'cunt'), **coral, cunnie, cunny, Delores, Döschen** (German, 'little box'), **fanny, flaps, furburger, fuzzy-bunny, Gizelle, hair-pie, home sweet home, honey-pie, jelly cave, jelly-roll, junioress, Kathy's pink surprise** (after a dish named thus, and his wife's name), **kitty, lei** (Italian, 'she, her'), **li'l pussy, liesje** (Dutch, Lizzie and *lies*, 'groin'), **Louis, love-box, love-nest, lunch, Magdalena** (after a very religious girlfriend), **Mary, Maxine, mick, money-pot, mouse, Ms Mary, muff, Muschi** (German, 'kitty-cat' and woman's name), **nether lips, pencil-sharpener, poussé** (fake French), **pretty little thing, princess, pussy cat, pussy-lips, Sally, Satchmo, satin doll, snutchie, squeeky, sugarbush, the Beave** (from *beaver*), **the Deep** ('she doesn't like it,' he added), **thing, tukso** (Tagalog, 'temptation'), **tunnel of love, tush, warm fuzzy, ying-yang** and **zouzoune** (his wife is French).

## Genital Pet Names Used by Homosexuals and Bisexuals

The remaining pet names are those provided by male and female homosexuals and bisexuals. Of 36 informants, 21 homosexual and bisexual men have pet names for their own penis namely: **Baby Huey, best friend, Chester, big dick, cock** (2), **cunt-leg, dick** (2), **John Henry** ('the steel-driving man'), **John Thomas, Junior, little thing, my ten inches, Omar, pee-pee** (2), **Peter, piece, pinky weenie, prick, Schwanz** (German, 'tail') and **willy.**

Pet names by homosexual males for their friends' penis: **cock, dick, handsome, little** (plus man's name), **love tool, Omar Junior, pee-pee, Peter, piece, pretty-dick, pussy, Schwanz, shlong, tally-whacker** and **tiny tot.**

Pet names by bisexual men for their friends' penis: **cock** (2), **cute, little pee-pee, dingus, joy-stick** and **junior.**

One lesbian reported a pet name for her own vulva: **Penelope** (she's of Greek origin).

Pet names by bisexual women for their own vulva are: **clit, my pussy-cat, pussy** (2), **tee-tee** and **vagina.**

Pet names by lesbians for their friends' vulva: **Fifi, little baby** and **Monique.**

Finally, pet names by bisexual females for their friends' vulva: **clit, flower, fur-patch, love-nest, pussy, tee-tee** and **vagina.**

## CONCLUDING REMARKS

As is the case with human beings who are attacked with derogatory names if they deviate from the norm – fat, skinny, short, tall, ugly, smelly, useless ones – body parts, too, are given deprecatory names if they deviate from the norm of a society or an individual.

Also, as in the case of people, there are many more negatively-valued (nasty) than positively-valued (nice) terms for body parts. From these large collections of negatively-valued data one can establish what the ideal, 'normal' person and body parts look like. From the nasty terms for penis and breasts, for instance, one can see what the ideal body parts should look like. As the nasty terms for penis predominantly deal with shortness, smallness, softness, uselessness, and illness, one knows that a so-called normal penis should be long, thick, hard, useful, and healthy. Similarly, the negatively-valued term for breasts tell us that 'normal' breasts should not be small, flat, dried up, fat, wrinkled, floppy or saggy.

So much for a first look at abusive, endearing and pet names for body parts that *all* people have, including cabinet ministers, royalty, journalists, chat-show hosts, pop stars, scholars and the ordinary man and woman in the street!

———————

How do you say 'Fuck you' in Jewish?
– *'Trust me.'*

What's the perfect woman like?
– *She's three feet tall, doesn't have any teeth, and the top of her head is flat so you can put your beer down on it.*

What do you call a faggot with a broken tooth?
– *An organ grinder.*

# ONE TOAST, NO FORK, NO SHEET: AN ITALIAN IMMIGRANT'S STORY

One day I'ma go to Detroit to da bigga hotel. Ina mornin', I go to da stair to eata breakfas'. I tella da waitress I wanna two pisses toast. She bringa me only one piss. I tella her I wanna two piss'. She say, 'Go to da toilet.' I say, 'You no understan', I wanna two piss' ona my plate.' She say, 'You betta no piss ona you' plate, you sonna-ma-bitch!' I'ma don't even know da lady and she call me sonna-ma-bitch.

Later I'ma go out to eat at da bigga restaurante. Da waitress bringa me spoon anna knife anna butta but no fock. I'ma tell her I wanna fock. She tell me, 'Everyone wanna fock.' I tella her, 'You no understan', I wanna fock ona table.' She say, 'You betta no fock ona table, you sonna-ma-bitch!'

Den I'ma go back to my room ina hotel, an' there isa no shits ona my bed. I calla da manager an' tella him I wanna shit. He tella me to go to da toilet. I say, 'You no understan', I wanna shit ona my bed.' He say, 'You betta no shit ona bed, you sonna-ma-bitch!'

I'ma go check outta an' da man at de desk say, 'Peace to you.' I'ma say, 'Piss on you too, you sonna-ma-bitch. I'ma go back to Italy!'

## COMMENTARY

The preceding tale is not a story ridiculing 'stupid' Italians, even though popular, trashy books misrepresent such material as 'Italian,' 'Polish' or 'Irish' jokes. In fact, the story has nothing whatever to do with Italians.

It is an example of *linguistic humour*, using the convenient and easily-recognized Italian accent as a vehicle to illustrate the tremendous semantic difference vowel length can make. The three minimal pairs, contrasting the long (:) with the short vowels, are the key to this tale:

| | | |
|---|---|---|
| *piece, peace* /pi:s/ | : | *piss* /pis/ |
| *fork* /fo:k/ | : | *fock* /fok/ |
| *sheet* /ši:t/ | : | *shit* /šit/ |

14

*Fork*, here the *r*-less variety Cf. /ka:/ 'car') and pronounced with an open *o*, may be an indication of the geographic background of the originator of this story since *fork* and *fuck* are phonetically not sufficiently close, in most English-speaking dialects, to be confused.

As speakers of English distinguish very well between long and short vowels, and are aware of the vulgar meanings of the mispronounced words, the story has to feature a character with a poor command of spoken English, such as a recent immigrant or a visitor to this country. Why not a Russian, Portuguese or Albanian? Because their accents are very difficult to represent in writing and are not recognized easily by most readers (or listeners). The Italian accent is widely mocked and is understood by the masses who circulate such tales. The protagonist in this human drama could have been speaking another frequently mocked accent, such as German ('I vant two shitt in mine bett') but the story would have lost much of its warmth and charm since the stereotypical German is not funny.

There is much more to this apparently simple 'joke.' We can *identify* with the poor fellow. The originator wanted just a simple laugh caused by the mispronounced naughty words, but I'm certain that sociologists, psychologists, folklorists and philosophers (not to mention Talmudic Scholars and Jesuits) could write long essays on the deeper meaning of this 'simple' tale. Without trying to wax philosophical, I do sense an illustration of the Human Condition, a tale of everyday misery, a Kafkaesque nightmare beneath this tale: the outsider, trying to communicate simple requests, is misunderstood again and again, but he is determined to get his wishes across. Yet, because of lacking communication, he is helpless. He becomes frustrated, resigns himself to being misunderstood, and capitulates, finally saying, 'To *hell* with it all! Who *needs* this hassle!? I'm going back to my kind, to where I'm understood.'

Surely, each of us has been in such frustrating situations where we simply could not get our point across, be it in a foreign country or with co-workers, a spouse, child or parent. Finally, after too much frustration, we become resigned and say, 'Oh, *fuck* it! (or civil equivalent) I'm leaving!' We can empathize with the tale's fellow-sufferer and therefore find it so appealing. It strikes a chord.

On a more mundane level, folklorists will recognize the ancient elements of folk tale and fairy tale: *three* events or situations (toast, fork, bedsheet) and *verbatim repetition* ('You no understan', I wanna . . . ' and 'You betta no. . . ., you sonna-ma-bitch') which have been used for thousands of years. Unwittingly, the originator of this modern 'urban folk tale' utilizes ancient story-telling techniques to which we respond subconsciously.

The only modern touches are the 'Peace' greeting of the desk clerk and especially the blasé, callous, smart-ass or so-what's-new? reply by the waitress, 'Everyone wants to fuck.' Other than that, and with a change of locale, this tale could have been told in England several hundred years ago.

---

What goes into thirteen twice?
– *Roman Polanski.*

What's brown and full of holes?
– *Swiss shit.*

Why don't Polish women use vibrators?
– *Because they chip their teeth.*

# LOUISIANANS DO IT BAYOUTIFULLY

(Reinhold Aman)

*Librarians do it quietly*
*Nurses do it with more patience*
*Judges do it with conviction*
*Lawyers do it in their briefs*
*Teachers do it with class.*

But . . .

Admirals do it fleetingly
Anaesthetists do it unconsciously
Artisans do it craftily
Atheists do it ungodly
Bankers do it interestingly
Beavers do it busily
Beginners do it startingly
Belgians do it bilingually
Ben does it gaily
Bigots do it intolerably
Brewers do it frothily
Buggers do it retroactively
Californians do it sharingly
Camels do it humpingly
Cannoneers do it ballistically
Canoeists do it with their paddle
Cardiologists do it heartily
Catholics do it rhythmically
Chinese do it inscrutably
Church Organists do it piously
Clerics do it religiously
Clockmakers do it watchfully
Columnists do it regularly
Compulsives do it neatly
Computer Operators do it bit by bit
Confectioners do it sweetly
Coprophiles do it shittily

Crocodiles do it tearfully
Crustaceans do it crabbily
Cunnilinguists do it succinctly
Cynics do it doggedly
Dentists do it inextricably
Dermatologists do it flakily
Divers do it muffedly
Dogs do it cynically
Dolphins do it flippantly
Donkeys do it asininely
Drill Operators do it boringly
Drinkers do it spiritually
Drummers do it differently
Dwarfs do it briefly
Einstein did it relatively
Electronics Engineers do it unbiasedly
Elephants do it with their trunk
Emperors do it majestically
Engineers do it mechanically
Eskimos do it coldly
Eunuchs do it uniquely
Exhibitionists do it flashily
Experts do it authoritatively
Field Marshals do it strategically
Frankenstein did it monstrously
Frenchmen do it frankly
Germans do it markedly
Gillespie does it dizzily
Grammarians do it punctually
Hairdressers do it permanently
Helen does it readily
Henry did it Thoreauly
Hermaphrodites do it selfishly
Hitchhikers do it with their thumb
Hotheads do it quickly
Illiterates do it indescribably
Indian Guides do it unerringly
Intellectuals do it with their head

Ivan did it terribly
Jakob & Wilhelm did it grimmly
Jewellers do it brilliantly
John Major does it conservatively
John Smith does it labouriously
Journalists do it reportedly
King Arthur did it knightly
Kings do it royally
Knights do it boldly
Lawbreakers do it offensively
Lensmakers do it objectively
Libertines do it freely
Magicians do it inexplicably
Martin Luther did it protestingly
Masturbators do it singlehandedly
Mathematicians do it figuratively
Michelangelo did it on his back
Miners do it with their shaft
Monoglots do it unilingually
Motorists do it exhaustingly
Mountaineers do it condescendingly
Muleteers do it with their whip
Musicians do it harmonically
Myopics do it shortsightedly
Necrophiles do it immortally
Nitwits do it unwittingly
Nouveaux Riches do it upwardly
Nudists do it barely
Nuns do it habitually
Oil Refinery Workers do it crudely
Oscar Wilde did it queerly
Osteopaths do it with their bone
Paddy Ashdown does it liberally
Paranoids do it suspiciously
Pavlov's Dog did it salivatingly
Peasants do it villainously
Pharmacists do it dopily
Pharyngologists do it throatily

Philosophers do it questionably
Pigs do it sloppily
Poles do it with polish
Post-menopausal women do it unbearably
Procrastinators do it later
Professors do it testily
Prostitutes do it tartly
Rabbits do it hairily
Railroad Engineers do it tenderly
Reporters do it sensationally
Roosters do it cockily
Rulers do it measuredly
Sadists do it smartly
Savages do it wildly
Schizophrenics do it twice
Semioticians do it symbolically
Septuagenarians do it weakly weekly
Sceptics do it incredibly
Snails do it slowly
Sodomites do it fruitfully
Soldiers do it patriotically
Speech Teachers do it orally
Spies do it under cover
Squirrels do it with their nuts
Statisticians do it averagely
Swimmers do it with a breaststroke
Swordsmen do it thrustingly
Sycophants do it praisingly
Tautologists do it repeatedly
Tom does it swiftly
Triplets do it thrice
Trumpeters do it hornily
Twins do it doubly
Undertakers do it gravely
Venus de Milo did it unarmedly
Whores do it trickily
Witch Doctors do it charmingly
Writers do it literally.

# PROVERBS IN GRAFFITI
# TAUNTING TRADITIONAL WISDOM

(Jess Nierenberg)

## I

For centuries, proverbs and proverbial formulae have been the bases in literature and folklore for wordplay and punning. These pithy, compact sentences are convenient and familiar, and provide frameworks for endless variation. Today, proverbs are parodied so often, and appear in their original form so infrequently, that their predominant current form *is* the variation or parody. This is not necessarily objectionable – if the sayings vary and evolve through traditional oral delivery – because any type of folklore must be able to change if it is to survive. More often though, proverb alteration is an important prop especially for 'popular' or mass-culture and mass-media writers. These writers – the newspaper editor composing a headline, the cartoonist seeking a caption, the pop singer writing for the adoring masses – all have in common a need for forcefulness and brevity. The pressures caused by deadlines and the inability to match the concise imagery of the proverb work to bring the proverb-as-framework into play. The most frequent usurper of the traditional proverb's power – and this is also true for other folklore genres, such as the folktale, riddle, or legend – is the advertising-copy writer. One need only skim through any magazine to find examples of what could be called 'proverb pollution': the perversion and trivializing of proverbs in order to sell products.

A consideration of proverb parody in traditional folklore should begin with the proverb itself. Like all current folklore, proverbs are constantly changing. Often, a proverb in oral

21

circulation evolves a tail, or tag line, that elaborates or plays upon the serious dictate of the proverb core. For example:

> I have other fish to fry (and their tails to butter)
> Every dog has his day (and a cat two Sundays)
> All things have an end (and a pudding has two)

The German proverb *Morgenstunde hat Gold im Munde* ('The morning hour has gold in its mouth', meaning that it pays to get up early) is now often heard as *Morgenstunde hat Gold im Munde und Blei im Arsch* ('. . . and lead in the arse'). Or it is simply abbreviated to *Morgenstunde hat Blei im Arsch*, leading the way for the formation of a new proverb from what was originally a parody.

Proverb parody in jokes are rare, and the only example discovered for presentation here is an item of 'metafolklore', a name for folklore that comments on other folklore; an example of metafolklore would be the proverbial definition of what a proverb is: 'The wit of one, the wisdom of many.' The following joking riddle plays upon the 'knock, knock' joke cycle and the proverb 'Opportunity only knocks once':

> Knock!
> Who's there?
> Opportunity!

The sub-proverbial genre of the Wellerism is a richer source of proverb parody. This form of folklore, named for Dickens's character Samuel Weller, consists of a proverb, a proverbial phrase, or any familiar saying, together with a sentence that describes an unusual, contrived situation. The original meaning of the proverb is distorted by the situation. For example:

> 'A little goes a long way,' as the monkey said when he shat over the brink of a precipice.
> 'No pleasure without pain,' said the monkey as he buggered the hedgehog.

Probably the most bizarre examples of proverb parody are reported by Richard Bauman and Neil McCabe in the *Journal of American Folklore* (1970). They write that altered proverbs were used as part of a ritual of induction into a pseudo-religious LSD-cult. The 'Litany' consists of quotations of Zen poetry topped off by altered epigrams and proverbs. The verse was chanted by a leader, and the top-off proverb line was solemnly repeated by a chorus. Some of the intoned lines were:

> Void will be void (Boys will be boys).
> A niche in time is thine (A stitch in time saves nine).
> You'll rush in where angels fear to tread (Fools rush in where angels fear to tread).

## II

During the last twenty years we have seen a flood of books and articles on the now-popular subject of graffiti. Many worthwhile scholarly articles have also appeared, making it possible to distinguish different types of graffiti: urban, rural, ethnic, men's, women's, political, territorial, sexual, indoor, outdoor, bathroom graffiti, etc. It is essential, in the wake of this surge of scholarship, that any discussion of graffiti include a description of which type is being discussed, and, if possible, which folk-group is writing it.

Proverb parody occurs regularly in a certain type of graffiti, and that is specifically the type in university milieus. Such writings are found indoors and outdoors on walls on university campuses, in parts of cities with large student populations, and in other intellectual settings often associated with the university scene, such as cafés and folk- and jazz-music clubs. The inscriptions are usually complete sentences or short rhyming verses, and attempts are commonly made by the writers to be aphoristic, polemical, or comic. The folk-group to which this type of graffiti can be attributed consists mainly of students and professors, plus other hangers-on to the campus scene. This group definitely overlaps and has much in common with the 'limerick set', as described by G. Legman in his introduction to *The Limerick*. It is also true that this type of graffiti is not to be found among the same groups that do not appreciate limericks:

Limericks are not liked by, nor commonly to be collected among, workingmen, farm-hands, cowboys, sailors, and other classic oral sources . . . Except for the basic subject matter, non-college people simply do not find it easy to understand where the humor is supposed to reside in all the trick geographical rhyming and other purely formal and intellectual ornamentation of the limerick.

Like limericks, the graffiti produced by the college crowd are made up largely of cute and clever sayings, wordplays, puns, and the sending-up of literary, historical, and political figures.

Although most printed collections of graffiti, including this one, are made up exclusively of the cute and clever kind, it does not follow that only cute wall writings are worth collecting and studying. Unfortunately, precisely such an elitist, literocentric attitude is propounded in a popular study of graffiti:

Before turning away from this general spectrum of what graffiti is today, I would like to mention one more category of graffiti, and that is false graffiti.

There should be a button which reads KEEP AMERICA BEAUTIFUL – STAMP OUT PSEUDO-GRAFFITI, because there is a great deal of writing on walls which should not be there, and cannot be called graffiti in the pure sense of the word. These inscriptions are, ordinarily, one-line gags or jokes of low-level stuff of dubious origin. . . In fact, many of the scrawls one sees these days are merely traditional jests whose origins are from vocal currency – radio, TV, living room or cocktail party exchange . . .

After you have seen a great deal of graffiti, you almost instinctively know which are genuine and which are phonies and, therefore, mere defacings of a good surface. The true graffiti has style, a surrealistic, imaginative quality, a spontaneity you can feel even though the topic itself may now be stale . . . (Reisner 1971: 21–22).

The writer goes on to decry unimaginative 'poor punning' as 'childish, immature graffiti', and then to declare, 'In this category should be included too, I think, what is on the whole the massive bulk of graffiti – names, often just first names, scratched or gouged around here and there.' By these standards most ethnic graffiti, graphic graffiti (drawings), the graffiti gangs use to demarcate territory, Daniel Boone's 'Cilled a bar' engraving from 1760, and indeed the 'massive bulk' of wall writings, are not valid graffiti in 'the pure sense of the word' because they aren't written in an original style. It would be truer to claim the opposite, namely that the cute and clever sayings, which the writer praises as 'true' graffiti, represent only a small fraction of a broad spectrum. A concentration of humorous sayings from the walls is only a very selective view of graffiti. In reality, most outdoor graffiti are banal, crude, or repetitive, but certainly worthy of study, as a reading of Allen Walker Read's *Classic American Graffiti* (1977) proves. Similarly, indoor graffiti, especially in lavatories, are mostly homosexual invitations, yet it remains unlikely that we will soon see printed collections of such writings, simply because they would not sell.

## III

The following examples have been chosen as representative examples to illustrate the various themes and different forms of proverb parody. The categories into which the examples are grouped are not final or exclusive. Some altered proverbs in graffiti do not fit neatly into any one category, and some can have more than one meaning, as do traditional proverbs such as 'A friend in need is a friend indeed/in deed' or 'A rolling stone gathers no moss.'

In 1559 Pieter Breughel painted his famous 'Netherlandic Proverbs', in which at least 90 different proverbs and proverbial phrases, such as 'to hang your jacket on the wind', 'armed to the teeth' and 'the blind leading the blind' are graphically portrayed. Artists since then, capitalizing on the stark imagery of the proverb, have integrated proverbial scenes into wood-engravings, tapestry, emblems, cartoons, and other media. Continuing this tradition, the graffitist also graphically portrays a proverb using the medium of graffiti:

**ɘbiꙅ ɿɘʜƚo ɘʜƚ no ɿɘnɘɘɿǫ ꙅʏɒwlɒ ꙅi ꙅꙅɒɿǫ ɘʜT**

'The grass is always greener on the other side.'

Similarly, it is only in writing that the familiar phrase 'The pen is mightier than the sword' could be transformed into:

**The penis mightier than the sword.**

This pun has been traced by G Legman directly to Mark Twain (Legman 1976), and now enjoys currency as a graffito.

Because graffiti are written on public walls, the opportunity exists for written dialogue between graffitists. This form of graffiti has been dubbed 'sequential parody graffiti' by a folklorist from UCLA. (Longenecker 1977). This is a bulky title for what could also be called 'dialogue graffiti'. Here are some of the 'Notes and Queries' all based on proverbs, with each succeeding line by a different writer:

If at first you don't succeed –
  *suck, suck again*
  *change your major*
  *get rid of your ego and it won't matter*
  try cocaine – right on – all around my brain
  *get rid of your old man – it'll help*
  *ask God what she thinks*
  play the dulcimer – right on – so do I in Richmond
  *read the directions*
  'If at first you don't succeed, try, try again.' (UCB Folklore Archives)

Logic: Love is blind, God is love, Ray Charles is blind, therefore Ray Charles is God
  *Ray Charles is love*
  *No, God is Ray Charles*
  God = Love = Blind, Ray Charles = blind – disjointed statement
  Have you seen Ray Charles' new piano? Neither has he.
  'Love is blind.' (UCB campus, Dwinelle Hall, 1st fl. men's room, 2/80)
  Assholes Go Home
  *to Southern California*
  LA's OK

*Home is where the asshole is.*
'Home is where the heart is.' (UCB campus, Evans Hall, 10th fl.
men's room, 2/80)

There has been discussion within folkloristics over the relative value of the *text* of an item of folklore compared to the importance of the *context* in which the item is found. Two examples of latrinalia, or bathroom graffiti, which by definition occur in only one context, can be understood only in light of their context. It is context alone (a lavatory wall) that gives new meaning to:

If at first you don't succeed, try, try again. (UCB Folklore Archives)

A parallel example from West Germany:

*Not kennt keine Gesetze.* (Krotus 1970)

This is a modified version of the German proverb *Not kennt keine Gebot*, 'Necessity knows no law.' It took on a decidedly scatological meaning when it was written in a train lavatory, directly above the little metal sign that forbids the use of the toilet while the train is stopped in the station.

Seemingly nonsensical graffiti, the significance of which will later be discussed, attest to the strong urge in the graffitist to simply write, regardless of content and logic:

Opporknockety only tunes once.
'Opportunity only knocks once.' (Adler 1967)

A watched Proverb butters no parsnips.
*a buttered parsnip watches no proverbs either.*
*a buttered watch parsnips no proverbs.*
melted butter never watches parsnips.
a parsnipped butter proverbs no grunch but the eggplant
over there.
*a panned pars nips no butter.* (Read 1978)

The last item is taken from a written collection, and was presumably a graffiti dialogue when it was collected. Note the self-conscious proverb parody, and the way the words and formulae of two proverbs, 'Words butter no parsnips' and 'A watched pot never boils' are inextricably intertwined.

Our folk-group of university-affiliated people is traditionally involved in social and political movements. Proverbs used in their graffiti are manipulated to proclaim the views of these movements:

**No nukes is good nukes.**
'No news is good news.' (UCB campus, Life Science building, 1st fl. men's room, 2/80)

**Dow shalt not kill.**
'Thou shalt not kill.' (Feinberg 1978)

**A woman's place is in the House . . . and the Senate.**
'A woman's place is in the home.' (UCB campus, Wheeler Hall, 1st fl. men's room, 2/80)

**Blood is thicker than oil.**
'Blood is thicker than water.' (UCB campus, Evans Hall, ground fl. men's room, 2/80)

**Ronald Reagan is his own reward.**
'Virtue is its own reward.' (Adler 1967)

During the 1960s and 1970s the term 'counter-culture' was in use to describe the young people who termed themselves in graffiti as 'the people our parents warned us about' (UCB Folklore Archives). Although often very conventional unto themselves, they praised non-conformity and drug-taking through proverb parody:

**A friend with weed is a friend indeed.**
'A friend in need is a friend indeed.' (Kehl 1977)

**The best things in life are freaky.**
'The best things in life are free.' (Kehl 1977)

**The grass is greener on the other side of the border.**
'The grass is always greener on the other side.' (UCB Folklore Archives)

Alexander Pope's now proverbial social comment, 'To err is

human, to forgive, divine', is used by the graffitist who is frustrated by a world of technology:

> To err is human, but it takes a computer to completely fuck things up.
> (UCB Folklore Archives)

The act of writing graffiti releases pent-up libidinal thoughts and frustrations. There is an element of exhibitionism in graffiti, combined at least in lavatory graffiti, with the implied sadism of having a captive audience. Not surprisingly, more than one-third of the graffiti collected for this study are sexual. Most sexual proverb parody graffiti comment on more or less heterosexual issues; this is not true of the sub-genre of lavatory graffiti in general, in which up to 80% are homosexual comments and invitations. Here, however, other ageless themes such as chastity, contraception, and masturbation are brought out:

> Never pull off tomorrow what you can pull off today.
> 'Never put off until tomorrow what you can do today.' (UCB Folklore Archives)

> Chastity is its own punishment.
> 'Virtue is its own reward.' (Mockridge 1969)

> Blessed are the pure, for they shall inhibit the earth.
> 'Blessed are the meek, for they shall inherit the earth.' (UCB Folklore Archives)

> Chaste makes waste.
> 'Haste makes waste.' (UCB campus, Dwinelle Hall, 1st fl. men's room, 2/80)

> An orgasm in the bush is worth two in the hand.
> 'A bird in the hand is worth two in the bush.' (Reisner 1971)

> A pill a day keeps the stork away.
> 'An apple a day keeps the doctor away.' (Kehl 1977)

> A pill in time saves nine months.
> 'A stitch in time saves nine.' (Kehl 1977)

Less conventional sexual activities are also discussed:

**Practice makes pervert.**
'Practice makes perfect.' (Reisner 1971)

**A woman's place is sitting on my face.**
'A woman's place is in the home.'(UCB campus, Wurster Hall, women's room, 2/80)

**Children should be seen and not had.**
'Children should be seen and not heard.'(Kehl 1977)

**Better latent than never.**
'Better late than never.' (Reisner 1971)

**Spare the rod and spoil the drag race.**
'Spare the rod and spoil the child.' (Reisner 1971)

During a two-year stay in West Germany, I studied the university-milieu graffiti there, and added some examples of German proverb parody graffiti to my collection. Because of the difficulty in translating and explaining proverbs, and the near-impossibility of translating the resulting puns and parody, these few representative examples will have to suffice:

**Viele Köche verderben . . . das Küchenmädchen.**
'(Too) many cooks spoil . . . the kitchen-maid.' (Krotus 1970)

**Lieber 'ne Blinde im Bett als 'ne Taube auf dem Dach.**
'It's better to have a blind woman in your bed than a deaf one on your roof.' (Sochatzy 1982). From the original proverb 'It's better to have a sparrow in your hand than a pigeon on your roof,' derived from the wordplay on *Taube* meaning 'pigeon' and 'deaf woman'.

**Der Student geht so lange zur Mensa bis er bricht.**
'The student keeps going to the university cafeteria until he vomits.' (Schmude 1982). From the original *Der Krug geht so lange zum Brunnen, bis er bricht,* 'The pitcher keeps going to the (water) well until it breaks.' Wordplay on *brechen* 'to break': 'to vomit'.

An anonymous writer argued that, 'the only difference between philosophy and graffiti is the word "fuck".' If this kind of folk philosophy differs in form from conventional philosophy, there are still arguably truths – honest and direct as always in folklore – to be found on public walls. It would not do any harm to take the advice,

> A closed mouth gathers no foot.
> 'A rolling stone gathers no moss.' (Kehl 1977)

The saying ' Behind every great man there's a woman' comments on the dependence of men on women. The following re-working of the phrase can be interpreted to either insult the proverbial woman behind every great man, or to comment on the fallibility of great men:

> Behind every great man there's an asshole.
> (UCB Folklore Archives)

Among the examples of philosophical graffiti, different 'schools of thought' can be discerned. One school, as seen through the use of proverbs and proverbial formulae, is characterized by cynicism and an every-man-for-himself attitude:

> Crime pays – be a lawyer.
> 'Crime doesn't pay.' (UCB campus, Boalt Hall [the College of Law building], 1st fl. men's room, 2/80)
>
> Crime pays, but you've got to be careful. (UCB Folklore Archives)
>
> If at first you don't succeed, cheat! (Reisner 1971)

In a more pessimistic vein:

> If at first you don't succeed, you're average. (Kehl 1977)
>
> Behind every silver lining there's a dark cloud.
>
> 'Behind every dark cloud there's a silver lining.' (Kehl 1977)

## IV

What is the message of these altered proverbs? Many people believe, as Sigmund Freud did, that there is such a thing as 'harmless' wit, and would point to the foregoing examples as proof of such. But the truth is that all humour, including seemingly trivial wordplays and puns, is steeped in aggression and is far from 'harmless'. The distortion of a familiar fixed-phrase is inherently aggressive against the conformity of saying the expected words in the expected order in the expected context. ' All word-play distorts familiar usage, and *distortion is a form of aggression*.' (Feinberg 1978) Further, there is the aspect of proverbs which represents conventional, respectable, traditional wisdom, and the parodist can show defiance by sneering at these. So it is not only the formulaic nature and conciseness of proverbs that make them appealing, but also their proud and didactic stances, which are easy targets.

And to what end does the graffitist so aggressively tear into the proverb? What is the message the graffitist is consciously or unconsciously communicating? Part of the answer can be found simply by analyzing the act of writing graffiti. In psychoanalytical literature writing is usually associated with an underlying smearing complex, arising from the urge, prematurely repressed through toilet training, to play with and smear faeces. Faecal substitutes, such as clay or finger-paints, are used by children to satisfy this urge, and, in short, writing and printing are seen as an adult extension of this trait. As curious as it may sound, the writing-defecation equation is supported by traditional folklore. Alan Dundes, making this same point in 'Here I Sit – A Study of American Latrinalia' (1975), quotes an oft-collected graffito that is surprisingly popular:

> Those who write on shithouse walls
> Roll their shit in little balls.
> Those who read those words of wit
> Eat the little balls of shit.

In other words, those who consume words are consuming symbolic faeces, and those who write words are manipulating or expelling it. This scatological graffito makes the same point:

> *Malerei ist fein und zierlich*
> *Aber nicht an diesem Ort*
> *Wo der Finger dient als Pinsel*
> *Und der Arsch als Farbdepot.*
> Painting is refined and delicate,
> But not in this place,
> Where the finger serves as paintbrush
> And the ass as paint repository.
> (Timidior 1912)

Dundes follows this equation out of the bathroom and on to the printed page, suggesting that filling a blank page with prose is motivated by the same urge:

> The writing-defecation equation suggests that the academic motto 'publish or perish', an oicotypal example of what might be termed the alternative structure proverb (cf. 'do or die', 'put up or shut up', 'fish or cut bait', etc.) may be 'shit or get off the pot' in symbolic disguise. One might remember that scholars are first supposed to amass great quantities of data from which they are expected to 'get stuff out regularly'. (Dundes 1975)

That's really putting the *caca* in *cacademic*! For males, it's just a short theoretical flush from there to what Legman has called ' the Male-Motherhood of Authorship' (1968), characterized by men 'leaving a mark' in the world with the publication of their 'brainchild', invariably dedicated to the wife, without whose patience, dedication, and co-operation the realization of the book would not have been possible. The point to be made here in respect to graffiti is that the graffitist, by writing dirty words and defiant slogans on public walls, is dirtying what was clean with writing, and in this sense graffiti is unconsciously a rebellious act.

Of course, on a conscious level too, writing on walls is a recalcitrant act. The graffitist is well aware that he or she is not supposed to write there, for not only is it implicitly forbidden by toilet training, but it is also overtly forbidden by those who own the walls and wish to keep them clean. Often there is a sign in the public lavatories asking that users refrain from writing on the walls, which probably, owing to the anti-authoritarianism inherent in graffiti, has the opposite of the desired effect. Equally futile is the threat of fines in some areas for writing on the walls. The frustrated owner sometimes sets up a blackboard in the corner as an area designated for graffiti, but this, too, is doomed to fail, for it contravenes the illicit character of the game and advertises itself as naked co-optation.

Finally, if the act of writing graffiti is defiant, the content is accordingly unsubmissive. Folk epigraphers regularly use taboo or dirty words, or at least use them more emphatically and with greater frequency than they are used in conversation, and otherwise do their best to show disrespect for famous people and the conventions of society and language.

Our graffitist, so busy rejecting all mores, can conveniently add a (further) dimension of defiance to his act by resolutely altering the proverb, the embodiment of the values he is scorning. The proverb may be manipulated towards a direct rejection of the perceived social comment; hence, crime *does* pay, but 'you've got to be careful' or else 'be a lawyer'. Virtue is no longer its own reward, but rather 'Chastity is its own punishment'.

More frequently, the proverb is used as a vehicle for an unrelated message, and the alteration does not speak directly to the apparent truth in the original saying. ('The best things in life are freaky', or 'To err is human but it takes a computer to completely fuck things up'.) But there is still satisfaction to be had by altering the 'conformist' phrase in order to use taboo words, refer directly to taboo subjects such as excrement, or express 'non-conformist' truths. That such satisfaction is gained can be proven by the nonsensical, seemingly innocuous examples of 'Opporknockety only tunes once' and 'A watched proverb butters no parsnips', etc. The message denoted is only ' I have toyed with a proverb', but we may infer the unseen sneer that goes with this kind of 'message' graffiti.

## V

The graffitist puts the cart before the horse and leaves it for all to see. Unlike the professional writer, the graffitist is revolting against more than the 'rules of language'. Proverbs represent logic and rationality, conformity and standards of propriety. The message of our individual writing on a public wall is one of direct or indirect renunciation of such ideals. Whether the proverb is used to lend an air of authority and legitimacy to the graffiti by 'letting the rhetorical power of the genre rub off on them' (Bauman & McCabe 1970), or the inscription contains a direct rebellion, as in 'If at first you don't succeed, cheat!' and 'Behind every silver lining there's a dark cloud', or if the rebellion is only implied, as in the nonsensical examples, graffitists inevitably intensify their messages by using proverbs and proverbial formulae.

---

Why did God make come white and urine yellow?
– *So that Italians could tell if they were coming or going.*

Did you hear about the flasher who wanted to retire?
– *He changed his mind and decided to stick it out another year.*

What's a concubone?
– *A male concubine.*

Who was the first soft-drink manufacturer?
– *Adam. In the Garden of Eden, he made Eve's cherry pop.*

Who was the first carpenter?
– *Eve. She made Adam's banana stand.*

# THE POETRY OF PORKING

(Joel Oppenheimer)

## A PREFATORY NOTE

this is a 'found poem,' which was discovered some fifteen years ago in *Slang and Its Analogues*; this wonderful dictionary, which was compiled at the turn of the last century by J S Farmer and W E Henley (of 'invictus' fame), and reprinted as one paperback volume by Arno Press in 1970; it appeared on remainder counters in the mid-seventies, whence i snatched my copy.

i had heard that there were three or four words the OED would not spell out – if memory serves, *fuck, cunt, arse*, and one other i can't recall – and, after having looked up *fuck* and *cunt* and failed to locate them, i began searching. *cunt* was easy, since i vaguely remembered that it was listed as 'monosyllable' in the OED. there it was in Farmer & Henley also – eight and a half columns of ways to say the word without saying it – and i promptly stole some of the terms to use in 'Monosyllable Poem', one of *The Woman Poems*, a volume i was writing at the time.

later, bored, my fingers idly straying o'er the book, i decided to try to find *fuck*. it was hidden under 'Greens'; i can assure you this took no less than serendipity to find. i have done no editing, revising, or playing around, save to repeat the entire phrases, group by group, and to break the lines by phrases. it is wonderful read aloud.

henniker, new hampshire 1984

to have, get, or give one's greens – to enjoy, procure, or confer the sexual favour said indifferently of both sexes.

36

hence, also, on for one's greens
    (amorous and willing)
after one's greens
    (in quest of the favour)
green-grove
    (the pubes)
green-grocery
    (the female pudendum)
the price of greens
    (the cost of an embrace)
fresh greens
    (a new piece)

derived by some from the old scots' *grene*: to pine, to long for, to desire with insistence; whence *greens*: longings, desires. but in truth, the expression is a late and vulgar coinage. it would seem, indeed, to be a reminiscence of *garden*, and the set of metaphors – as *kail*, cauliflower, *parsley bed*, and so forth – suggested thereby.

## I

to be all there but the most of you
to be in abraham's bosom
to be up one's petticoats
to be among one's frills
to be there
to be on the spot
to be into
to be up
to be up to one's balls
to be where uncle's doodle goes
to be among the cabbages

## II

to dance the blanket hornpipe
to dance the buttock jig
to dance the cushion dance
to dance the goat's jig
to dance the mattress jig

to dance the married man's cotillion
to dance the matrimonial polka
to dance the reels o' bogie
to dance the reels o' stumpie
to dance to the tune of the shaking of the sheets
to dance with your arse to the ceiling
to dance with your arse to the kipples

## III

to go ballocking
to go beard-splitting
to go bed-pressing
to go belly-bumping
to go bitching
to go bum-fighting
to go bum-working
to go bum-tickling
to go bum-faking
to go bush-ranging
to go buttock-stirring
to go bird's-nesting
to go buttocking
to go cock-fighting
to go cunny-catching
to go doodling
to go drabbing
to go fleshing it
to go flesh-mongering
to go goosing
to go to hairyfordshire
to go jock-hunting
to go jottling
to go jumming
to go leather-stretching
to go on the loose
to go motting
to go molrowing
to go pile-driving
to go prick-scouring

to go quim-sticking
to go rumping
to go rump-splitting
to go strumming
to go twatting
to go twat-faking
to go vaulting
to go wenching
to go womanizing
to go working the dumb oracle
to go working the double oracle
to go working the hairy oracle
to go twat-raking
to go tummy-tickling
to go tromboning
to go quim-wedging
to go tail-twitching
to go button-hole working
to go under-petticoating

## IV

to have, or do, a bit of beef
to have, or do, a bit of business
to have, or do, a bit of bum-dancing
to have, or do, a bit of cauliflower
to have, or do, a bit of cock
to have, or do, a bit of cock-fighting
to have, or do, a bit of cunt
to have, or do, a bit of curly greens
to have, or do, a bit of fish
to have, or do, a bit on a fork
to have, or do, a bit of fun
to have, or do, a bit off the chump end
to have, or do, a bit of flat
to have, or do, a bit of front-door work
to have, or do, a bit of giblet pie
to have, or do, a bit of the gut-stick
to have, or do, a bit of the cream-stick
to have, or do, a bit of the sugar-stick

to have, or do, a bit of jam
to have, or do, a bit of ladies' tailoring
to have, or do, a bit of meat
to have, or do, a bit of mutton
to have, or do, a bit of pork
to have, or do, a bit of quimsy
to have, or do, a bit of rough
to have, or do, a bit of sharp-and-blunt
to have, or do, a bit of stuff
to have, or do, a bit of split-mutton
to have, or do, a bit of skirt
to have, or do, a bit of summer cabbage

## V

to have, or do, or perform, the act of androgynation
to have, or do, or perform, a ballocking
to have, or do, or perform, a bit
to have, or do, or perform, a lassie's by-job
to have, or do, or perform, a bedward bit
to have, or do, or perform, a beanfeast in bed
to have, or do, or perform, a belly-warmer
to have, or do, or perform, a blindfold bit
to have, or do, or perform, a bottom-wetter
to have, or do, or perform, a bout
to have, or do, or perform, a brush with the cue
to have, or do, or perform, a dive in the dark
to have, or do, or perform, a drop-in
to have, or do, or perform, a double fight
to have, or do, or perform, an ejectment in love-lane
to have, or do, or perform, a four-legged frolic
to have, or do, or perform, a fuck
to have, or do, or perform, a futter
to have, or do, or perform, a game in the cock-loft
to have, or do, or perform, a goose-and-duck
to have, or do, or perform, the culbatizing exercise
to have, or do, or perform, a grind
to have, or do, or perform, a hoist-in
to have, or do, or perform, a jottle
to have, or do, or perform, a jumble-giblets

to have, or do, or perform, a jumble-up
to have, or do, or perform, an inside worry
to have, or do, or perform, a leap
to have, or do, or perform, a leap up the ladder
to have, or do, or perform, a little of one with t'other
to have, or do, or perform, a mount
to have, or do, or perform, a mow
to have, or do, or perform, a nibble
to have, or do, or perform, a plaster of warm guts
to have, or do, or perform, a poke
to have, or do, or perform, a put
to have, or do, or perform, a put-in
to have, or do, or perform, a random push
to have, or do, or perform, a rasp
to have, or do, or perform, a ride
to have, or do, or perform, a roger
to have, or do, or perform, a rootle
to have, or do, or perform, a rush up the straight
to have, or do, or perform, a shot at the bull's eye
to have, or do, or perform, a slide up the board
to have, or do, or perform, a squirt-and-a-squeeze
to have, or do, or perform, a touch-off
to have, or do, or perform, a touch-up
to have, or do, or perform, a tumble-in
to have, or do, or perform, a wet-'un
to have, or do, or perform, a wipe at the place
to have, or do, or perform, a wollop-in

## VI

to have, or do, a back scuttle
to have, or do, a buttered bun
to have, or do, a dog's marriage
to have, or do, a knee-trembler
to have, or do, a perpendicular
to have, or do, an upright
to have, or do, a matrimonial
to have, or do, spoon fashion
to have, or do, a st george

# VII

to play at all-fours
to play at adam-and-eve
to play at belly-to-belly
to play at brangle-buttock
to play at buttock-and-leave-her
to play at cherry-pit
to play at couple-your-navels
to play at cuddle-my-cuddie
to play at hey gammer cook
to play at fathers-and-mothers
to play at the first-game-ever-played
to play at handie-dandie
to play at hooper's hide
to play at grapple-my-belly
to play at horses-and-mares
to play at the close-buttock-game
to play at cock-in-cover
to play at houghmagandie
to play at in-and-in
to play at in-and-out
to play at irish-whist
to play at where-the-jack-takes-the-ace
to play at the loose-coat-game
to play at molly's-hole
to play at pickle-me-tickle-me
to play at mumble-peg
to play at prick-the-garter
to play at pully-hauly
to play at put-in-all
to play at the-same-old-game
to play at squeezem-close
to play at stable-my-naggie
to play at thread-the-needle
to play at tops-and-bottoms
to play at two-handed-put
to play at up-tails-all

## VIII

to adam and eve it
to blow the groundsels
to engage three to one
to chuck a tread
to do
to do it
to do 'the act of darkness'
to do the act of love
to do the deed of kind
to do the work of increase
to do 'the divine work of fatherhood'
to feed the dumb-glutton
to get one's hair cut
to slip in daintie davie
to slip in willie wallace
to get jack in the orchard
to get on top of
to give a lesson in simple arithmetic
to give a lesson in addition, subtraction,
multiplication, and division
to give a green gown
to go 'groping for trout in a peculiar river'
to go face-making
to go to durham
to go to see a sick friend
to have it
to join faces
to join giblets
to make ends meet
to make the beast with two backs
to make a settlement in trial
to play top-sawyer
to put it in and break it
to post a letter
to go on the stitch
to labour lea
to tether one's nags on
to nail twa wames thegither

to lift a leg on
to ride a post
to peel one's end in
to put the devil into hell
to rub bacons
to strop one's beak
to strip one's tarse in
to grind one's tool
to grease the wheel
to take on a split-arsed mechanic
to take a turn in bushey-park
to take a turn in cock-alley
to take a turn in cock-lane
to take a turn in cupid's-alley
to take a turn in cupid's-corner
to take a turn in hair-court
to take a turn in the lists of love
to take a turn in love-lane
to take a turn on mount pleasant
to take a turn among the parsley
to take a turn on shooter's-hill
to take a turn through the stubble
to whack it up
to wollop it in
to labour leather
to wind up the clock

## IX

to get an arselins coup
to catch an oyster
to do the naughty
to do a spread
to do a tumble
to do a back-fall
to do what mother did before me
to do a turn on one's back
to do what eve did with adam
to hold up one's tail
to turn up one's tail

to get one's leg lifted
to get one's kettle mended
to get one's chimney swept out
to get one's leather stretched
to lift one's leg
to open up to
to get shot in the tail
to get a shove in one's blind eye
to get a wet bottom
to get what harry gave doll
to suck the sugar-stick
to take in beef
to take nebuchadnezzar out to grass
to look at the ceiling over a man's shoulder
to get outside it
to play one's ace
to rub one's arse on
to spread to
to take in and do for
to give standing room for one
to get hulled between wind and water
to get a pair of balls against one's butt
to take in cream
to show a bit
to give a bit
to skin the live rabbit
to feed one's pussy
to trot out one's pussy
to lose the match and pocket the stakes
to get a bellyful of marrow pudding
to supple both ends of it
to draw a cork
to get hilt and hair
to draw a man's fireworks
to wag one's tail
to take the starch out of
to go star-gazing on one's back
to study astronomy on one's back
to get a green gown

to have a hot pudding for supper
to have a live sausage for supper
to grant the favour
to give mutton for beef
to give juice for jelly
to give soft for hard
to give a bit of snug for a bit of stiff
to give a hole to hide it in
to give a cure for the horn
to give a hot poultice for the irish toothache
to pull up one's petticoats to
to get the best and plenty of it
to lie under
to stand the push
to get stabbed in the thigh
to take off one's stays
to get touched up
to get a bit of the goose's-neck
to get a go at the creamstick
to get a handle for the broom

# X

to have connection
to have carnal intercourse
to have improper intercourse
to have sexual intercourse
to know carnally
to have carnal knowledge of
to indulge in sexual commerce
to go to bed with
to lie with
to go in unto
to be intimate
to be improperly intimate
to be familiar
to be on terms of familiarity with
to have one's will of
to lavish one's favours on
to enjoy the pleasures of love

to enjoy the conjugal embrace
to embrace
to have one's way with
to perform connubial rites
to scale the heights of connubial bliss
to yield one's favours
to surrender
to give one the enjoyment of one's person
to use benevolence to
to possess

---

While a lion is drinking at a river, a gorilla sneaks up from behind and slips him a Liberace. He then takes off, with the lion in hot pursuit. The ape jumps into a hunter's tent, puts on a safari outfit, dons a pith helmet, grabs the *Daily Star*, and sits down to read. The lion follows the ape's scent to the tent, sticks his head in and asks: 'Did you see a gorilla come through here?' – The ape replies, 'You mean the one that fucked the lion in the ass?' – 'My God!' roars the lion, 'It's in the papers already?'

# TRADE NAMES OF AMERICAN CONDOMS

(Sir Maurice Sedley, *Bart*)


One afternoon, while idly perusing some condom catalogues, the large variety of condom trade names caught my attention, and after classifying them, I found that all fifty-two names could be subsumed under five general categories:

(1) AGGRESSION: N=6, 11.5%; (2) HEDONISM: N=29, 55.5%; (3) MORPHOLOGY or SHAPE: N=6, 11.5%; (4) NEUTRALITY: N=7, 13.5%; (5) PROTECTION or SECURITY: N=4, 8%.

Considering the rampant egocentric male-chauvinist piggery and hostility-aggressiveness which has long characterized typical American masculine sexual attitudes and behaviour – the former exemplified by the classic '4F' joke, *viz.* First American Male: 'In my sexual relationships, I always follow the 4F Rule.' Second AM: 'What's that?' First AM: 'Find 'em, feel 'em, fuck 'em, forget 'em.' – the latter exemplified by the snide question-and-answer puzzle, *viz.* Q: 'Describe the typical American male's sexual behaviour in five words.' A: 'Slam! Bam! Thank you, Ma'am.' – it was surprising to find such a small percentage of obviously aggressive condom trade names in the observed set.

An analysis of the six identified aggressive condom trade names indicates that all of them imply a potential violent physical assault on the female body.

**Bold 45:** The 45 refers to a .45 calibre handgun which a behatted, jean-clad female is playfully pointing, thus setting herself up as a 'target' to be 'hit' or 'scored upon' by the male's 'gun'.

**Conquerer:** A robust, horn-helmeted Viking with a murderous-pointed spear in hand just waiting for the opportunity to go into action.

**Musketeer:** Shades of Cyrano de Bergerac, Athos, Porthos, Aramis and D'Artagnan which transfer military aggressiveness into sexual aggressiveness, tacitly directing it against the female body as a fortress to be taken by assault.

**Olé:** A lover as a matador out to overpower or vanquish female sexuality by means of a skilful but deadly assault.

**Rough Rider:** A triple entendre indicating various types of assault, *viz.* (1) studs on the condom to increase its roughness when in use; (2) the female body as enemy to be vanquished by a sabre-waving, war-whooping cavalryman charging up the 'San Juan Hill' of Venus; (3) rider of a spirited but not totally manageable mount, determined to tame the mount.

**Superstud:** A female as breeding-stock assaulted for hire.

## Categorized List of Fifty-Two Condom Trade Names

| AGGRESSION | NEUTRALITY |
|---|---|
| Bold 45 | Fourex |
| Conquerer | Jellia |
| Musketeer | Naturals |
| Olé | Plus |
| Rough Rider | Prime |
| Superstud | Sta-Tex |
| | Wrinkle Zero-0 |

| MORPHOLOGY or SHAPE | PROTECTION or SECURITY |
|---|---|
| Conture | Convoys |
| Hugger | Guardian |
| Nu-Form | Shields |
| Pointex | Trojan Guardian |
| Slims | |
| Trojan-Enz | |

HEDONISM
Adam's Rib
Apollo
Black Cat
Cavalier
Embrace Her
Eros
Excita
Fiesta (coloured)
Fetherlite
Geisha Thins
Gold Circle Coins
Hotline
Jade (green, blue,
   gold, red)
Longtime
Nuda
Patrician
Peacock
Pleaser
Ramses
Saxon
Scentuals (musk, banana,
   strawberry, lime)
Score
Sheik
Skinless Skin
Stimula
Sultan
Tahiti
Texture Plus
Tingla

Little Dickie Cavity, the 'intellectual' television host, likes to make fun of Germans and their language – something Mark Twain did long ago, and far better. On the 'Tonight Show' of 28 October 1981, Dick Cavett told Johnny Carson that the German word for 'condom' is *Geschlechtsgliedbeschützer*. Balls! This contrived word literally means 'sex-member-protector' which no German-speaking person ever uses.

The four most common terms are *Gummi* 'rubber,' *Pariser* 'Parisian' (cf. English 'French letter'), *Fromms* (a brand named after its producer and ironically meaning 'pious, religious'), and *Überzieher* 'overcoat,' lit. 'over-puller,' something one pulls over one's penis. Other common terms are *Präservativ* 'preservative,' ie, something that protects one from getting VD, and the learned *Kondóm*.

Euphemisms for condom abound. Among the most popular are *Gummihandschuh* 'rubber-glove', *Gummimantel* 'rubber-overcoat', *Luftballon* 'balloon', *Nahkampfsocke* 'close-combat sock', *Pfeifenpullover* 'pipe-pullover' (pipe = penis), *Schwanzfutteral* 'tail-sheath', *Tropfenfänger* 'drop-catcher', and *zweite Haut* 'second skin'.

# ITALIAN BLASPHEMIES

(Giuliano Averna and Joseph Salemi)

Swearing and cursing are very common in Italy. Although the practice is impolite, and a sin in the eyes of religion, most Italians – regardless of their social level – frequently use blasphemy. Perhaps centuries of religious domination, both temporal and spiritual, in extremely close proximity to the central power of the Catholic Church, have driven them to it.

We are all well aware that there are many ways to exorcize something hostile or inimical to us. When we speak of death we are exorcizing it. When we talk more or less freely about homosexuality we often relieve our anxiety concerning the subject. When we refer casually to the signs of age on our bodies, we exorcize our fear of old age and perhaps death itself. In a similar manner, Italians have traditionally cursed and sworn as a means of verbal exorcism, and they continue to do so today.

For centuries blasphemy was the only way of escaping the legal, moral, and inquisitorial power of the priest, the confessor, and the preacher. In the midst of a life of privations these clerics told, counselled, and ordered the wretched majority of the populace to continue suffering and obeying in the hope of a heavenly reward. Meanwhile, the dream of a land flowing with milk and honey was realized daily in the castles and palaces of the rich.

God is clearly the catalyst for the majority of these blasphemies, but we also find expressions that mention Christ, the Madonna, the sacraments, and so on. I have listed here about one hundred expressions in which God's divinity is blasphemed or insulted, along with some euphemisms. They have all been collected from the Italian language and its various dialects.

51

Abbreviations:

| | |
|---|---|
| *cal.* dialect of Calabria | *rom.* dialect of Rome |
| *emil.* dialect of Emilia | *sic.* dialect of Sicily |
| *ferr.* dialect of Ferrara | *tosc.* dialect of Tuscany |
| *lig.* dialect of Liguria | *ven.* dialect of Veneto |
| *mil.* dialect of Milan | *venez.* dialect of Venice |
| *par.* dialect of Parma | *veron.* dialect of Verona |

**Dio assassino!** *That assassin of a God!*

**Dio 'ssasino!** (*ven.*) *That assassin of a God!*

**Dio beco!** (*ven.*) *Horned God! God with a beak!* This imprecation refers to the horns of cuckoldry. The blasphemy would then have the same force as **Dio cornuto!** *Beco* (Venice, Veneto) and *becco* (standard Italian): 'he-goat'; 'beak'; 'cuckold'.

**Dio bestia!** (*ven.*) *That beast of a God!*

**Dio bestialone!** *That big beast of a God!* In Italian the suffix *-one* is a pejorative addition that connotes both largeness and derogation.

**Dio birbo!** (*ven.*) *That rascal of a God!*

**Dio bonino!** (*tosc.*) *Good God!*

**Dio brigante!** (*ven.*) *That bandit of a God!* Brigands and bandits have always been a part of Italian life.

**Brigante de Dio!** (*ven.*) *That bandit of a God!*

**Dio brutt!** (*emil*) *Ugly God!*

**Dio brutto!** (*ven.*) *Ugly God!*

**Dio buono!** *Good God!*

**Dio campanile!** (*venez.*) *That bell tower of a God!* In Venice and Veneto, *campanile* is also pronounced *canpanile*.

**Dio cane!** *That dog of a God!*

**Dio can!** (*ven.*) *That dog of a God!*

**Can de Dio!** (*mil.*) *That dog of a God!*

**Dio 'hane!** (*tosc.*) *That dog of a God!*

**Dio can-arino!** (*ven.*) *That canary of a God!* This and the following two items are examples of verbal stops, designed to suggest *cane* 'dog'.

**Dio can-oro!** (*ven.*) *That singer of a God!*

**Dio can-tante!** (*ven.*) *That singer of a God!*

**Dio cara!** (*ven.*) *Dear God!*

**Dio caro!** (*ven.*) *Dear God!*

**Dio cangi!** (*lig.*) *Dear God!*

**Dio cornuto!** *Cuckolded God!* See **Dio beco!**

**Dio culattiere!** (*venez.*) *That sodomite of a God!* From *culatta*, the rump, the seat of the pants.

**Dio fiol!** (*ven.*) *That son of a God!*

**Dio ladro!** (*ven.*) *That thief of a God!*

**Dio mamma!** (*ferr.*) *That mother of a God!* 'Mother' in this imprecation should be understood in the literal sense, not as the shortened form of *motherfucker*, a meaning which the term almost always carries in American malediction.

**Dio madonna!** (*ven.*) *That Madonna of a God!*

**Dio mas-cio!** (*ven.*) *That boy of a God!* Another verbal stop, perhaps to suggest the term *mascalzone* 'rogue, blackguard'. *Mas-cio* also means 'pork.'

**Dio mat!** (*ven.*) *That madman, lunatic of a God!*

**Dio nimale!** (*par.*) *That animal of a God!*

**Dio nimel!** (*par.*) *That animal of a God!*

**Dio porco!** *That pig of a God!*

**Dio porc!** *That pig of a God!*

**Dio prete!** *That priest of a God!* In a country with a strong anticlerical tradition the term *prete* is often used pejoratively. *Strozzapreti* ('It strangles priests') is the name of several Italian dishes. Apparently, this term is derived from the priests' reputation of being big, greedy eaters. Naming a dish *strozzapreti* thus indicates that it is so generous that it would even choke a priest.

**Dio sagrasco!** (*rom.*) *That sacrament of a God!* (**Dio sacramento!**) The sacrament referred to is the Eucharist or Christ's body. **Corpo di Cristo!** ('Body of Christ') is a very old Italian blasphemy, and there was no end of trouble in Italy when the Church switched from Latin to the vernacular in its services. Instead of saying *Corpus Christi* in Latin during Mass, priests had to say *Corpo di Cristo*, thus introducing blasphemy into the heart of the liturgy.

**Dio sagraschio!** (*rom.*) *That sacrament of a God!*

**Dio sagrataccio!** (*rom.*) *That sacrament of a God!*

**Dio sagrato!** (*rom.*) *That sacrament of a God!*

**Dio sborà!** (*ven.*) *God jacked-off! That jacked-off God!* From *sborar(e)* 'to ejaculate'.

**Dio serpente!** (*ven.*) *That snake of a God!*

**Dio sarpente!** (*ven.*) *That snake of a God!*

**Dio scanpà!** (*ven.*) *God ran off!*

**Dio scapà da lett!** (*par.*) *God escaped from bed!*

**Dio scapà da lett senza scarpi!** (*par.*) *God escaped from bed without shoes!* This and the following forms help reduce the blasphemy by their expansion.

**Dio scapà da lett senza gambe!** (*par.*) *God escaped from bed without legs!*

**Dio scapà da lett in bicicletta!** (*par.*) *God escaped from bed by bicycle!*

**Dio sallarga!** (*rom.*) *Expanding God!* Euphemism for **Dio sacramento!**

**Dio s'allarga!** (*rom.*) *Expanding God!*

**Dio serenella!** (*rom.*) *Cloudless God!* Nineteenth century, military use.

**Dio travo!** (*ven.*) *That beam of a God!*

**Dio impalato!** (*tosc.*) *That shafted God!*

**Dio rospo!** (*tosc.*) *That toad of a God!*

**Orco Dio!** (*ven.*) *That pig of a God!* Euphemism for **Porco Dio!**

**Orco zio!** (*ven.*) *That pig of a God!* Double euphemism; *zio* 'uncle'.

**Per Dio!** *By God!*

**Per brio** (*par.*) *By God!* Euphemism.

**Par bio!** (*par.*) *By God!* Euphemism.

**Pebbio!** (*rom.*) *By God!* Euphemism.

**Peddio!** (*rom.*) *By God!* Euphemism.

**Peddio sagranne!** (*rom.*) *By holy God!* Euphemism.

**Peddio sagraschio!** (*rom.*) *By holy God!* Euphemism.

**Peddio de legno!** (*rom.*) *By wooden God!* Euphemism.

**Perdio sagrato!** (*rom.*) *By holy God!*

**Perdio santo a le bocie!** (veron.) By holy God playing bocce! *By holy bowling God!* Blasphemy reduced by expansion.

**Pardia!** (*veron.*) *By God!* Euphemism.

**Par die!** (*veron.*) *By God!* Euphemism.

**Par didedi!** (*veron.*) *By God!* Euphemism.

**Pardiu!** (*cal.*) *By God!* Euphemism.
**Pardeu!** (*cal.*) *By God!* Euphemism.
**Parbeu!** (*cal.*) *By God!* Euphemism.
**Pardena!** (*cal.*) *By God!* Euphemism.
**Perdena!** (*cal.*) *By God!* Euphemism.
**Perdeu!** (*cal.*) *By God!* Euphemism.
**Porco Dio!** *That pig of a God!*
**Porco zio!** *That pig of a God!* Euphemism.
**Porki dia!** *That pig of a God!* Euphemism. Sometimes *porco* is written with a *k*, just as *cazzo* 'prick' is seen written as *kazzo*.
**Porco diose!** (*ven.*) *That pig of a God!* Euphemism.
**Porco madono!** (*ven.*) *That pig of a Madonna!*
**Sacher Dieu!** (*mil.*) *Holy God!* Cf. the French *sacrebleu!* where *bleu* 'blue' is a phonetic euphemism for *Dieu* 'God'. In French, however, *sacre* has retained the original double meaning of the Latin *sacer*: 'holy' and 'accursed'. Thus *sacrebleu!* means 'damned God!'
**Sangue di Dio!** *Blood of God!*
**Sangue de Dio!** (*ven.*) *Blood of God!*
**Sangue de bio!** (*rom.*) *Blood of God!* Euphemism.
**Sango de bio!** (*par.*) *Blood of God!* Euphemism.
**Sanguanon de bia!** (*mil.*) *Blood of God!* Euphemism.
**Sandiocan!** (*ven.*) *That dog of a holy God!*
**Santo Dio!** *Holy God!*
**Santi dia!** (*sic.*) *Holy God!*
**Santu dia!** (*sic.*) *Holy God!*
**Vaca dio!** (*ven.*) *That cow of a God! That whore of a God!* – *Vaca* 'cow' is one of the most common insults meaning 'whore'.
**Zio porco!** (*ven.*) *That pig of a God!* Euphemism.
**Zio cane!** (*ven.*) *That dog of a God!* Euphemism.
**Zio can!** (*ven.*) *That dog of a God!* Euphemism.
**Zio schitaron!** *That chickenshitting God!* – *Schito* is 'chickenshit', and *schitarar* means 'to defecate', especially in reference to chickens.

# TAXONOMIC PORNITHOLOGY
# RULES FOR THE NAMING OF
# EGREGIOUS AND OBSCENE BIRDS

(Douglas Lindsey)

Synthetic pornithology is the development of avian labels to describe varieties of human appearance and behaviour. The obligate brevity of ornithologic nomenclature suggests relationship with both the one-liner and the pun, but these mechanisms do not adequately explain the range of possibilities of synthetic ornithology as a form of humour.

Labelling a person as a bird is not new. All academicians are familiar with the pejorative labelling of a visiting lecturer as a **turkey**, and more than a few of us have, on occasion, legitimately earned the designation. Tucson, by virtue of its far southern location in the Great American Desert, is the destination in winter of great flocks of migrating **snowbirds**, for which more precise speciation is possible. The **greater greenbacked snowbird** is enthusiastically welcomed as a 'winter guest'. The **lesser sooty snowbird**, on the other hand, is regarded as a pest. Euphemistically labelled as a 'transient' (we try, with scant success, to encourage it to move north to Phoenix or west to Los Angeles), it befouls the shrubbery in Armory Park, clutters the lobby of the main post office with its queues before the General Delivery window, and roosts at night around campfires along the tracks of the Southern Pacific Railroad. The **lesser sooty snowbird** is accompanied by the **common stench**, always the **lesser stench**, and sometimes the **greater stench** as well.

The serious and systematic recording of collections of synthetic ornithologic species is a hobby of regrettably few devotees, and I see little prospect for a boom in the field.

56

Perhaps the potential for proliferation of enthusiasts is greater in the field of taxonomic pornithology, a subset within synthetic ornithology which permits the venting of a pornithologic bent while offering immunity against accusation of public flatus in polite company. Provided, of course, that such verbal farting is accomplished in accordance with the recognized rules of a creative scholarly endeavour.

The first basic rule of taxonomic pornithology is: *it's got to sound like a bird.* You can give it a bird's name, literally, or a bird's name which is twisted slightly or punned. You can make it a bird by using avian-specific anatomy, or avian-specific functional nomenclature. You can get away with many designations which are bird-related, but not avian-specific. And when you get rolling, you can make derivations which are ornithologic only by association and context. Which brings up the second basic rule of taxonomic pornithology: *if it passes for a bird, it is.* The risk of overstretching the immunity from obscenity is your own. If you provided an adequate context, and it flies, it's a bird. If it doesn't fly, you are stuck with mouthing dirty words.

An example of the use of legitimate bird names is the **perpetual grouse**. A takeoff from the **prothonotary warbler** is the **penitentiary warbler**, also known as the **stool pigeon**. A medical example is the **intertriginous thrush**. But the archetypical example of the technique is the **extramarital lark**.

Tweaking the bird name just a little offers more possibilities. The **ruffled spouse** is often found in association with the **extramarital lark**. The **great American craven** proliferated enormously during the war in Vietnam – to such numbers that large flocks migrated to Canada. The **California condom**, once thought to be near extinction as the result of advances in steroid chemistry, is now making a comeback as result of the threats induced by herpes and Acquired Immune Deficiency Syndrome (AIDS).

The door is open. If there is a *junco*, there is a **junkie**. If there is *cardinal*, there is **venial**. If there is a *phoebe*, there is a **feelie** and a **freebie**. If there is a *curlew*, there is a **curfew**. If there is a *barred avocet*, there must be a **disbarred advocate**. There are *buzzards and bustards*: surely there must be **bastards**, and the **yellow-bellied bastard** is one of my earliest and most faithfully recurring species.

In terms of avian-specific anatomy, my base type is the **buff-tinted due-bill**. Pornithologic? Of course. Bad enough that the scoundrel is dunning me for his ill-gotten gains; he is doing it on *off-colour, laid* paper! But my favourite is the **right-winged sanctimoner**, or **phallusy**. A **phallusy** is the public claim to potency and prowess which does not exist. A prime example is the man who stuffs two socks into the crotch of his bathing trunks to draw incredulous stares from the babes at the beach.

Anatomical terms which are not avian-specific require a little more caution. After all, there are non-avian species which can be described in their own right as full-breasted, sharp-clawed, and twitchy-tailed. But the **pearl-throated dowager** will pass (there is a bird known as the *dowitcher*), as will the **mink-breasted Yentl**, the **bald gay**, and the **red-nosed lush**.

Many legitimate avian species are labelled by particular function or behavior. If there is a *gnatcatcher*, there is surely a **nitpicker**. If there is a *roadrunner*, there must be a **street-walker**. A good example of functional identification with birds is the **accidental flycatcher**, also known as the **impaled prepuce** or the **zippered thatch**.

There is a bird known as the *wandering tattler* which gives rise to the **village gossipmonger** and the **suburban fink**. The **all-night bed-thrasher** warms many hearts, two at a time. If there is a *white wagtail*, there must be a **black wagtail** and a **yellow wagtail**. The last implies oriental origin, so it may be called the **transverse snatch**. There is, indeed, a bird known as the *white-collared seedeater*, which translates to the **executive gay**. There is a *greater frigate bird*: why not a **lesser upyurass**?

Incidentally, the adjectives that ornithologists use are amusing in their own right. There are birds which are *fulvous*, *ferruginous* and *flammulated*. Another legitimate ornithologic adjective is *frugiverous*, meaning 'fruit-eating', which leads to the **frugiverous reciprocating gay**, implying an all-male 69.

Let us note some examples of how far out we can stretch and distort a few common and uncommon birds.

There is a Mexican bird, little known to most of you, named the *copper trogon*, from which we can deduce the **pink-ribbed Trojan** and the **rubber Ramses**. For those of you who are not from the western side of the Atlantic, I might explain that *Trojan* and *Ramses* are popular brands of condoms in the United States.

The *robin* is a common bird, but I have been able to make little of it.* The **hooded robin** comes to mind. Probably extinct now, but occasionally sighted of yore in Nottingham Forest. Hardly pornithologic, but **cradle robin** offers some opportunities: **Nabakov's Lolita** and **Polanski's nemesis**.

The *swallow* provides much food for thought. Physicians and many patients are quite familiar with the **barium swallow**. There is a real bird known as the *violet green swallow*, certainly a nauseating combination, perhaps to be labelled the **imminent barf**. There is a little hummingbird which is also purple and green; surely it can be labelled the **regurgitant sip**.

And then, of course, there is the **deep-throated swallow**, known also as the **plum-headed gag** or **common puke**. For the ladies who perhaps feel put upon in such matters, I offer the **avid busheater**, the **long-billed muff-diver**, the **cunning lingus**, and for those whose tastes in the matter are utterly feminine, the **Lapland gull**. But my favourite in this group is the **limber-tongued gash hawk**.

Of course, if one is serious about ornithology or pornithology one needs a 'field guide' – how to identify the species if you don't have it in your grubby little hand, or in your bush. Let me tell you how to spot the **limber-tongued gash hawk**. He hangs out in the singles bar. He comes early, but never stays late. He comes alone, but never leaves alone. He sits at the little table in the corner, where he can look out over the whole room. He orders a huge pitcher of beer, from which he drinks, in single gulps, spaced at long intervals. Most of the time he just sits there, licking the foam from his eyebrows. His favourite beer? *Slits*.

---

*Editor's Note*: The robin is Wisconsin's State Bird. Its Latin name is *Turdus migratorius*.

Another bird familiar to, and beloved by almost all of you, is the *cock*. Male homosexuals think there is absolutely nothing finer than the **cock**. Virtually all admitted and practising heterosexuals think highly of the **cock**, too. And in certain forms, the **cock** is esteemed by the lesbian. Take the **many-splintered woodcock**. Few would take it, willingly, even though it featured heavily in the romantic novel *Love is a Many-splintered Thing*. But how about the **burnished woodcock**, also known as the **mahogany dildo**?

A minor variety, but worth some discussion, is the **matutinal peecock**, also known as the **early-morning hard** or **uriniferous cock**. Morphologically it is identical with the familiar **erogenate cock**; in fact, in museum specimens – skinned and dried – the two are indistinguishable. Behaviourally they are quite different. The **erogenate cock** struts proudly during the pre-mating ritual. The **matutinal peecock** is shy, almost secretive, sometimes recognizable only by the tenting of its cover. You seldom get to examine one closely unless you have a domesticated specimen. It often runs away when it is uncovered; you might even say that it disappears when it is flushed.

Of course there are a few of the species of **cock** which work night shifts and sleep in the daytime. This is the **vespertine peecock** which, on occasion, can be confused with the **great horny owl**.

Also familiar to you are *tits* and *boobs*. I read an article once on the feeding habits of *great tits* – nutritional requirements and food intake. This has confused me; I had always thought it was the other way round. Incidentally, I have never quite understood the alleged erogenous importance of size in **great tits**. It seems that simply quoting the numbers 38-27-35 is supposed to be an instant turn-on. More important, I think, is form, feel and flavour. There are **silicone tits**; their flavour is poor.

**Boobies** are closely related to **tits**. The corollary to the *great tits* is the **saddle-bag booby**, usually observed in the **shrouded** variety. The **lesser shrouded booby** is also known as the **cross-your-heart bra**, and the **least shrouded booby** is also known as **Frederick's pastie**.

Finally, there is a group of birds known as the *ani*. If you will permit me the presumption that the singular of *ani* is *anus*, this opens up other avenues for exploration. There is the **patulous anus**, and the **petulant anus**. There is the **pendulous anus**, also known as the **prolapsed pile**. And, of course, there is the **fiery-red anus**, known also as the **tabasco twat, el ano salsado**, or simply the **Mexican heartburn**.

Let me encourage you to take up the hobby of taxonomic pornithology. If you think I have exhausted the possibilities, think again. Find an unusual adjective, and then hang it on a bird. For example, the **obvallate fink** is synonymous with the **penitentiary warbler**. Find an unusual noun, and use it. The word *rantallion* is British slang for a man whose balls hang lower than his pecker. Obviously, then, there are *two* avian species: the **short-dinked rantallion**, and the **big-knockered rantallion**. Find both noun and adjective. The **jubate merkin** is a female pudendum with hair like a horse's mane. The **irrumant agomphyx** is the nice little old lady – the *cute* nice little old lady – who takes her teeth out before she goes down on you. When you return the favour, you can identify the **poliotic pubis**, also known as the **mottled muff**, the **bespotted beaver**, or the **salt-and-pepper snatch**. And how about the **preprandial pallion**, literally translated as 'a little piece before lunch,' also known as the **quickie**?

Taxonomic pornithology does have a redeeming virtue during air travel. Sit in the middle seat of a wide-bodied jet. Stare up at the ceiling, stare all around you, looking for pornithologic species. Move your lips slowly while naming species, without uttering a sound. Then smile, giggle, and occasionally break out in hearty laughter. Soon the flight attendant will find other seats for the passengers on your right and left, and you can stretch out and sleep, or continue to amuse yourself without abusing yourself, all the way across the Atlantic.

# CHAIN LETTER FOR WOMEN ONLY

This letter was started by a woman like yourself, in the hopes of bringing relief to other tired and discontented women. Unlike most chain letters, this one does not cost anything.

Just send a copy of this letter to five of your friends who are equally tired and discontented. Then, bundle up your husband or boyfriend, send him to the woman whose name appears at the top of the list, and add your name to the bottom of the list.

When your name comes to the top of the list, you will receive 16,877 men – and one of them is bound to be a hell of a lot better than the one you already have !

Do not break the chain . . . Have faith! One woman broke the chain and got her own SOB back. At this writing, a friend of mine had already received 184 men. They buried her yesterday, but it took three undertakers 36 hours to get the smile off her face and two days to get her legs together so they could close the coffin.

*You must have faith!*

Signed

**A Liberated Woman**

# A WARD OF WORDS:
# MEDICAL GROUP NOUNS

('Sue Ture')

## A

an acceleration of radiation therapists
an augmentation of plastic surgeons
an aura of neurologists

## B

a bag of anaesthesiologists
a blast of haematologists
a block of anaesthesiologists
a body of anatomists
a body of pathologists
a box of gynaecologists
a broth of bacteriologists
a bruit of vascular surgeons
a bundle of cardiologists

## C

a callous of podiatrists
a cast of orthopaedists
a chest of pulmonologists
a circle of neurosurgeons
a clap of venereologists
a clot of cardiologists
a coil of gynaecologists
a colic of neonatologists
a complex of psychiatrists
a compulsion of psychiatrists
a convergence of ophthalmologists

a convulsion of neurologists
a corpus of gynaecologists
a corpus of urologists
a cortex of neurosurgeons
a cough of thoracic surgeons
a coupling of cardiologists
a crash of lab technicians
a croup of paediatricians
a culture of virologists
a cusp of cardiologists

## D

a desiccation of gerontologists
a diffusion of respiratory therapists
a disorder of psychologists
a dissection of vascular surgeons
a dodder of geriatricians
a dotage of gerontologists

## E

an echo of cardiologists
an ejaculation of urologists
an emission of radiation therapists
an epidemic of virologists
an eructation of gastroenterologists
an evacuation of proctologists
an eyeful of ophthalmologists

## F

a fellation of head nurses
a fissure of proctologists
a flash of radiographers
a flatulence of gastroenterologists
a flutter of cardiologists

## G

a gag of laryngologists
a gasp of respiratory therapists

a giggle of nurses
a graft of plastic surgeons
a group of haematologists
a gumma of syphilologists
a gutful of gastroenterologists
a gyrus of neurosurgeons

**H**

a hive of allergists

**I**

an implantation of plastic surgeons
an invasion of cardiologists

**J**

a joint of orthopaedists

**K**

a knot of surgeons

**L**

a lay of venereologists
a labour of pregnant women
a leak of urologists
a lobe of endocrinologists
a loop of nephrologists

**M**

a macula of ophthalmologists
a malformation of geneticists
a mass of oncologists
a murmur of cardiologists
a mutation of geneticists

**N**

a neoplasia of oncologists
a nidus of neurologists
a Nissl of neuropathologists

a nucleus of cytologists

## O

an obfuscation of gerontologists
an outbreak of epidemiologists

## P

a perfusion of pump technicians
a phthisis of pulmonologists
a pile of proctologists
a plexus of neurologists
a ptosis of plastic surgeons
a pucker of assholes
a pyramid of nephrologists

## Q

a quadrant of abdominal surgeons

## R

a rash of dermatologists
a recuperation of patients
a resonation of radiologists
a retort of biochemists
a revision of plastic surgeons

## S

a scope of endoscopists
a scrub of interns
a snatch of gynaecologists
a spasm of gastroenterologists
a stutter of speech pathologists
a stream of urologists
a sublimation of psychiatrists
a sufferance of patients

## T

a tincture of pharmacists
a ton of bariatricians

a tremor of neurologists
a tumescence of sexologists

## W

a wave of electroencephalographers

---

*A Recipe for the Festive Season*
TURKEY WITH POPCORN DRESSING
(Serves 12)

One 15-lb Turkey                    2 Cups Bread Crumbs

Seasonings                          2 Diced Onions

1 Can Bouillon                      3 Cups Popcorn

½ Cup Diced Celery

**Method:** Stuff turkey and bake at 325° about five hours, or until the popcorn blows the turkey's ass clear across the room.

# TALK DIRTY TO ME:
# SEXY SLOGANS ON BUTTONS, CARDS,
# T-SHIRTS, AND RUBBER STAMPS

(Reinhold Aman)

Age is not important unless you're a bottle of wine
Another brillyant mind diztroyed by the edukashun sistum
Are you going to come quietly or do I have to use earplugs?
Asshole by birth
Bastard by choice
Beat me, whip me, pay me
Bitch by birth
Blink if you're horny
Can I touch your tits?
Come near me and I'll kill you
Condoms are for faggots
Could I see Uranus tonight?
Cunning Linguist
Deep, considerate, sensitive, and horny
Do you find it hard getting up in the morning?
Don't even think about fucking me
Don't even think of fucking me without a condom
Don't try to understand me, just fuck me
Don't you dare even *think* about me when you masturbate
Eat well, stay fit and die anyway
Eat, Fuck, Kill
Everyone needs to believe in something. I believe I'll have
   another beer
51% Sweetheart, 49% Bitch
Fuck me or I'll try to sell you insurance
Fuck that shit
Fuck you very much

Give me a quarter or I'll touch you
Go fuck yourself. Without a condom
Haven't I fucked you before?
How can I love you if you won't lie down?
How can I say I ♥ you if you're sitting on my face?
How do you spell relief? M-a-s-t-u-r-b-a-t-e
I accept tits
I can't decide whether to commit suicide or go bowling
I don't give a shit. I don't take any shit. I'm not in the shit
    business
I don't have PMS, I'm always a bitch
I don't like your negative attitude, asshole
I don't want a love affair, just a blow job
I have trouble remembering names. Can I just call you 'asshole'?
I know you just want to get into my pants but I already have
    an asshole in there
I love every inch of you
I love it when you talk dirty
I may be fat but you're ugly, and I can diet
I need more money and power and less shit from you people
I smell shit. Is there an estate agent in here?
I think I could fall madly in bed with you
I tried to drown my troubles, but my husband learned to swim
I want to thank all the little people who kiss my ass
I wish your breasts were larger
I wish your penis was harder
I would look good on you
I wouldn't eat you if you were between two slices of bread
I wouldn't fuck her with your dick
I'd like to get something straight between us
I'd like to see more of you
I'd slap you but shit splatters
I'll only hurt you in the end
I'll shake your hand when you take it out of your nose
I'll sleep with you if you're rich or famous
I'm a worthless piece of shit. What's your excuse?
I'm not deaf, I'm ignoring you
I'm not prejudiced. I hate everybody

I'm not your fucking therapist
I'm witty, charming, handsome and above average in length
I've seen better heads on a pimple
If I can't find true love then I'll settle for sex with you
If I was alone on an island with you I'd masturbate
If you don't smoke, I won't fart
If you like sex and travel, go take a fuckin' hike
Inconsiderate, insensitive bastard seeks girl like you to dominate
It's a bitch being a queen
It's American to be pissed off
It's been lovely but I have to scream now
It's been so long since I've had sex I can't remember who gets
    tied up first
Kiss me or I'll masturbate
Life is a bitch and so am I
Liquor in the front, poker in the rear
May I fuck you?
Mother Teresa is better in bed than you are
My condoms or yours?
My erections last longer
Never too drunk to fuck
No more Mr Nice Guy: on your knees, bitch
Not all men are fools. Some are bastards
Not recently laid
OK. But wash it first
Only a bastard like me could love a bitch like you
Seven days of sex makes one weak
Sex is like everything else. If you want it done properly, you
    have to do it yourself
Shit happens
Shut the fuck up
Shut up and fuck
Sit on my face and let me eat my way to your heart
Size does count
Spread your legs
Stop staring at my tits
Survey says: go fuck yourself
Talk dirty to me

The difference between genius and stupidity is that genius has
  its limits
The meek shall inherit shit
There are many ways to say I LOVE YOU but fucking is the best
There is nothing like lipstick around my dipstick
Those of you who think you know everything are very annoy-
  ing to those of us who do
Too ugly to live, too weird to die
Trust me. I'm a lawyer
Usually I'm very caring. As for you, I don't give a shit
Vicious power-hungry bitch
Warning: I scream when I come
We cheat tourists & drunks
When I want any shit out of you I'll squeeze your head
When I'm with you I feel crazy. Sometimes I feel nuts
Whip me, beat me, bite me, come all over my body. Tell me
  you love me, then get the fuck out
Who farted?
Who needs this shit?
Who says I'm too short?
Who the fuck do you think you are?
Winning isn't everything but losing sucks
With friends like you who needs enemas?
Women who come close to me know how big I can be
You are who you eat
You come first
You have to fuck a lot of frogs in order to find a prince
You must be walking backwards. All I see is an asshole
You piss me off, you fuckin' jerk
You're the reason my children are so ugly
You're ugly and your mother dresses you funny
Your breasts are bigger than your brains
Your face or mine?
Your lips are too rough for oral sex
Your penis reminds me of the man I love
Your silly appearance coupled with your vile and unctuous
  skin makes you truly nauseating
Yuck Fou

# WINDY WORDS

(Bob Burton Brown)

*Said a printer pretending to wit:*
*'There are certain bad words we omit.*
*It would sully our art*
*To print the word F . . .,*
*And we never, oh, never, say Sh . . . '*

Some people, especially women over forty, simply cannot bring themselves to use the word *fart*. Although this word may be an appropriate Anglo-Saxon expression commonly used in many classics of English literature and today in every school playground by even the most innocent of children, it is still considered vulgar and offensive to some. So it has become a tradition to invent all sorts of euphemisms – most of them silly or childish – to cover the subject; anything to keep from coming right out and saying it.

**Arsenal cheer:** an oral imitation of a sputtering fart, employed to take advantage of a psychological moment which will not wait for the passage of the real thing. Used as a euphemism in 'Are you giving me the raspberry?' or 'Here's what I think of that . . . '

**bark:** a sharp report, as in a 'barking' gun, makes this a natural for a noisy passage of gas: 'Are you barking for your supper or because of it?'

**barking spider:** a gentle, family-type expression to cover the subject in reasonably good humour: 'Did I hear a barking spider just now?' or 'It's about time to call the exterminators; those barking spiders are back again'.

**beanie:** a childish choice, relying on supposition of cause for its identification rather than the end result, as in 'Was that your beanie I heard?' or 'Do your beanies always smell that bad?'

**borborygmus:** internal farting, the rumbling sounds made by the movement of gas in the intestine, as in a 'growling stomach', 'belly noise', 'gut mumblings', when your stomach 'talks to you'. Not very useful, since most people will not understand what you are talking about.

**bowel howls:** not really delicate enough to qualify, but nicely descriptive for locker-room talk.

**breaking wind:** very descriptive, and perhaps the most acceptable euphemism in literary circles, but terribly stilted, and dated, too.

**cushion creeper:** a muffled fart that seems never to end, and lingers – both the sound and the smell – in, around, and on the soft cushion of an over-stuffed chair or sofa. 'I've had about all of your cushion creepers I can take.'

**cutting the cheese:** how folks in Indiana describe it when someone lets out an especially stinky fart, as in 'Cutting the cheese is not allowed in the living room'.

**elephant on my back:** an announcement that you are about to let one rip, intended to dupe some gullible fool (or child) into making an innocent inquiry or investigation – then 'getting it' with a well-timed blast. Also, one may inquire of a suspected culprit, 'Is there an elephant on your back?'

**exterminal gas:** a quasi-technical term to describe particularly smelly expulsions of intestinal gas – the kind that could exterminate you, or provide overwhelming evidence that the expulsor is afflicted by something terminal.

**flatulence:** gas with class; whatever fancy folks blow out their ass.

**flatus:** farts with status; a puff of wind; gas generated in the stomach or bowels.

**gas** or **gassy:** mothers who have traditionally had real difficulty bringing themselves to use four-letter Anglo-Saxonisms often prefer to describe flatulence as 'gas', as in 'You seem to be awfully gassy today' or 'Was that your gas?' or 'I just passed some gas'.

**house frog**: another family-type term often used to explain the situation nicely, as in 'What was that?' – 'Just a house frog.' – 'OK.' An outside equivalent may be found in the question 'Who stepped on that frog?' or 'Is that damned frog loose again?'

**it**: an all-purpose term for whatever four-letter word we feel we must avoid, as: 'OK, you guys, which one of you did it?' or 'It just slipped out.'

**one**: what prudes call an expulsion of intestinal gas, as in 'Did you just let one?' – 'Yes, and that *one* is enough.'

**one-cheek sneak**: when little boys in short trousers fart while seated on a flat wooden bench or chair.

**pain**: an indirect reference to discomforting flatulence, sometimes used as a euphemism, as in 'Did you just have a pain?' Or as a confession in 'That was a terrible pain I got rid of.'

**painting the lift**: after you have just let a real stinker in a lift (thinking you are all alone) and somebody gets on at the next floor, you wrinkle up your nose and say, 'They must have just painted this lift.' In our family we all know what it means when one of us asks, 'Who painted the lift?'

**passing gas**: pretty straightforward, but it always reminds me of a cartoon I saw once of several bicyclists pedalling past a petrol pump held by a disappointed service-station attendant on a lonely highway in the desert, with the caption 'Passing Gas'.

**pets**: what French-Canadians call farts; and farting is called 'petting' – not because they are fond of it, and not to be confused with the pawing of eager lovers; short for the French word *péter*, meaning 'to crack, to explode, to break wind' – in other words, a French fart.

**poop**: a noun, used as a euphemism for anything that comes out of the anus; often a term of pseudo-endearment, as in 'You old poop!'

**puff**: as in 'a puff of wind', exappropriated as a verb all too often, as in 'I hope all those beans we ate for supper don't make us puff all night.'

**pumping gas**: a childish euphemism for farting – a confusion of the kind of gas Daddy puts in his car with the kind he puts out of his rear end.

**raspberry:** the equivalent of 'an Arsenal cheer', a mouth-fart, used as an expression of derision to let others know that you are displeased with them. A spluttering noise made while sticking the tongue out, which translates: 'I fart on thee!'

**rattler:** a reverberating blast powerful enough to rattle cups and saucers, or, perhaps, even the windows and doors of rickety buildings – like army barracks.

**SBD:** the abbreviation for the worst kind of fart – the silent-but deadly; in medical circles, this is called a 'tacit' fart.

**shooting rabbits:** what one says when one hears a fart of unknown origin: 'Somebody is shooting rabbits!' or 'Are you the one that's been shooting rabbits all night?'

**silent horror:** a very smelly fart inflicted upon another without fair warning; illegal chemical warfare, something akin to mustard gas.

**smell** or **smelly:** too obvious to merit comment: 'Mummy, I let out a smelly.'

**snappers:** beans, for obvious reasons; also used to describe what happens after the beans have had a chance to work.

**sniffle:** the women and children in my ex-wife's family used this word, both as a noun and as a verb, to cover their flatulence as sweetly as possible. Personally, I never liked the term. On my side of the family a 'sniffle' was something we blew out of our nose.

**sputter:** sound imitations are sometimes useful: 'I've been sputtering (*or* spluttering) all day.' However, one can go too far with this if the imitation is too close to the real thing, as in 'Who just "sphtttttt"?'

**squeaking chair:** a clever way to bring the passage of gas to public attention, asking: 'Are you sitting in a squeaking chair?' or 'I think my chair squeaks.' A variation on this theme can be: 'Is there a mouse in here?'

**stepping on a frog:** if you have ever stepped on a frog, or can imagine the complaints the frog would make you if you did, no further explanation is necessary.

**stink** or **stinky:** boys let 'stinks' but nice little girls call theirs 'stinkies'.

**storm:** implies a strong and dangerous wind, invariably noisy, as in 'Is that your storm I hear?' – 'Yes, my stomach is really storming (*or* howling) today.'

**toot:** a mild euphemism for a particularly melodious fart.

**whiff:** a windy-sounding term that makes your meaning clear. 'Somebody just whiffed; I can smell it!' Variations: **whiffles** and **whiffling**.

**wind:** as in 'Was that your wind?' or 'Gosh, I feel windy today' or 'Standing downwind of you can be dangerous.' Sometimes referred to as a **howling wind**.

# THANK YOU FOR NOT FARTING

## HOW TO JUDGE PEOPLE BY THEIR FARTING STYLES

(L Herrera)

**Crafty** (*taimado*): The person who cuts one and then looks around as if somebody else had done it.

**Silly** (*tonto*): The guy who cuts farts when he's asleep and gets up to see who knocked at the door.

**Surprised** (*sorprendido*): Somebody who thought he was letting one out silently but has it come out thundering.

**Expert** (*perito*): The man who can tell his own from somebody else's even when they smell at the same time.

**Eloquent** (*elocuente*): The person whose farts make people gather around to listen.

**Honest** (*honrado*): The guy who cuts them loudly and openly.

**Lovesick** (*enamorado*): The bloke who delights in breathing his girlfriend's farts.

**Perspicacious** (*perspicaz*): The person who can tell by the smell what the perpetrator had eaten and the name of the restaurant.

**Good Businessman** (*comerciante*): The guy who lets farts in monthly instalments.

**Well-bred** (*educado*): The person who holds a fart even though he's all alone, just out of consideration for himself.

**Simpleton** (*simple*): The guy who cuts farts in the bathtub and gets a big charge out of the bubbles they make.

**Unlucky** (*desafortunado*): The individual who lets rip-roaring big farts.

**Cautious** (*precavido*): The bloke who lets them out gently so his shorts won't get torn.

**Musically Inclined** (*filarmónico*): The guy who can perform ascending and descending scales.

**Dumb** (*estúpido*): The bloke who enjoys somebody else's fart thinking it was his own.

**Joker** (*comodino*): The man who lifts his butt so he can cut one at will.

**Strategist** (*estratégico*): The person who knows how to disguise a fart by sneezing or making some other opportune noise.

**Curious** (*curioso*): When this bloke cuts a fart in a cane-bottom chair, he squats down to see which hole it came out.

---

Why did God make farts smell?
– *So the deaf can enjoy them, too.*

# A PHILOLOGIST'S PRAYER

(Robert St Vincent Philippe)

*Our Teacher who art in English,*
*Proper be Thy Noun;*
  *Thy Adverb come,*
  *Thy Will (and Shall) be done*
*In Pronouns as in Interjections.*

*Give us this day our Passive Verb*
*And forgive us our Prepositions,*
*As we Decline those who Conjugate against us.*

*And lead us not into Conjunctions,*
*But deliver us from Adjectives,*
  *For Thine is the Comma,*
  *And the Period,*
  *And the Colon, forever.*

                    *Amen*

# TAE THE MAN IN THE SCOATTISH DICSHUNIRY

*Dear Mistir,*
ah wiz doon at the Libry thither settirday since ah hud
nuchin tae dae lookin up the dirty words in the big dicshuniry
theyv goat doon there an ah saw this ithir big yin cod the
Scoattish nashinul dicshiniry thats the yin thit you wrote. So
thinks ah tae masel ahl hae a wee keek tae see whit yir sayin.
Anywiy whaur tae start so ah looks up 'fuck' bit its not there
but 'fud' is. That means buttocks but ah always thoat it wiz a
lassies cunt. That wiznae there eethir bit 'cuntack, cuntie' wiz
an it says that means The father-lasher bit ah dinnae ken whit
a faithir lashir is neethir. Mibay thats hiz faithir hittin him yit
wi his big black belt when hez auld an yir faithir says 'ya auld
cuntie.' Ah dinnae ken. Mibay its a cathlick thing. Anywiy ahm
sittin there wunderin whit nixt tae look up when it dond oan
me that it wiz jizt Scoattish words so ah thoat whit dirty words
di ye ken thi ur Scoaish. Then ah thoat aboot the gid auld
poyem we uset tae say a Thinfant skill [at the infant school
'kindergarten']. This is the poyum ah thoat aboot: Keech bum
toaly fart, aw went doon the public park. Keech bum couldnae
swim, toaly fart blew him in.
Ye ken that yin divint [don't] ye. Its a gid yin ay. Whit
a joab ah hud findin 'keech' in the book cause it wiz spellt 'kich'
bit anywiy it says an ah wrote it doon it means ordure,
excrement, filth or dirt of any kind. Well ah ask ye. Anybudy
kens that 'keech' is the stuff thats oan yir pants if ye dinnae
dicht [wipe] yir erse richt an 'kech' is whit happens when
sumebudy skites [slides] through dugs shite oan the pavement
an it lies fur a gid few days afore it rains. 'Keck' is dried up
keech an is darker broon. Well ah jizt hope ye read this in time
cause ah see ye hivnae 'toaly' yit or 'tooch' in the words. Ah
wid jist like tae tell ye ah think a toaly is bigger than a tooch
an a tooch is softer than a toaly an a toaly if its din ootside hiz
mair steam bit a gid tooch hiz mair flees [horseflies]. Ahl keep
gawin doon tae keep them in mind tae see whit ye say.

*Signed a Skill Laddy*

# A NEW EROTIC VOCABULARY

(Tim Healey)

Several years ago I became involved in some correspondence wherein I had referred to the 57 Varieties of synonyms for the penis. Someone wrote commending me on my erudition and I was insulted, writing back that '57 Varieties' was a generic term taken from Heinz's advertisements and that I knew many hundreds of terms for the lady's lollipop. The matter rested there, but ever since I have kept a note of whatever terms I come across for male and female sexual apparatus and related accessories and activities. My sources are mainly English and mainly from the nineteenth century, but there is a good deal of overlap, because, eg, *Fanny Hill* was just as popular a hundred years ago and reprints of Victorian underground literature are still selling well. This essay was first intended as introduction to a projected work to be called *A Dictionary of the Very Vulgar Tongue*, but I fear it will never be completed. So far I have about 1000 terms (in English) for 'penis', about 1200 for 'vulva', 800 or so for 'to have sexual intercourse' and nearly 2000 for 'prostitute', Several of these last were not originally English, but I understand that this is the state amongst harlots, as well as the words describing their activities. My collection continues to grow, and this article is offered as a foretaste of what astonishing variety of vocabulary is available and in the hope that it will inspire writers above the monotony of so many modern writers and speakers.

## CONCERNING THE NAMES FOR THE FEMALE SEXUAL PARTS

Apart from the 'venerable monosyllable' itself (**cunt, quim, gash, mot** ( = Fr. 'word,' ie the unnameable), **motte, twat, slit, pelt,** etc), the simplest words in common use for this 'nasty thing' (*c\*\*\** – a nasty word for a nasty thing: Grose) are those accepting the female sexual apparatus as a simple receptacle. These include **hole, cranny, crack, crevice, slit, slot, furrow, ditch, gutter, trench, gulley,** or **gulley-hole, chasm, gap, gape** (Ba'al-Peor, the old phallic god of the Carthaginians, literally translates as 'Lord of the Widely Open Vagina': I usually put it as God of the Gaping Gap), **gulf** (hence **gulf-oil**), **pit, placket** and many others. Of course, **vagina** – the official anatomical term is Latin for 'sheath', but the specialized use eg in the German *Schamscheide* is better translated as a colloquial 'shame-slit' rather than the exact literal 'shame-sheath'. Quite apart from the fact that the anatomical term is restricted and exact, **vagina** is not the same as any of these terms and bowdlerization only invites ridicule for precisely this reason.

Occasionally, the colloquialism acknowledges the functions of the part, as is seen with **Cupid's furrow, Fumbler's Hall** (*to fumble* is seventeenth-century *thrimbling*), **tunnel of love, happy cloister** (though this is mainly rhyming slang on **hairy oyster**), **baking pot**(where you keep a bun in the oven), **Gate of Life,** or **mine of pleasure**. Other references to function occur in **money-spinner, whetting-corne** (= grindstone), **grindstone, Lob's pound** (a hand quern), the **playground** or a **Gentleman's pleasure garden**. Most of these 'functional' terms are less succinct than the 'hole' terms and the last occurs also in the use of **gentleman's pleasure garden padlock** for an ST (= sanitary towel) which is also known as a **manhole cover** or **jamrag**.

The effects of rising eroticism alluded to in **dewy sheath** are summarized by the Arabs in the use of the phrase 'Eblis has caused a moisture to flow.' Eblis – 'Adam's first wife was she' (Goethe) – was the original Devil-Woman, and we have recognized the effects of the flow of this letchwater by referring to the **lady's water-box, -course, -gap, gate** (no connection with recent break-ins), **-engine, -works** or **-mill**. The tendency is also remembered in the phrases to **grease the wheel, to do a wet 'un, to get a wet bottom** and **to do, have** or **perform a bottom-wetter,** namely **to do a turn on one's back,** or, as the Creoles put it, **to count shingle-pegs.**

Then there are the euphemisms used in more respectable literature, or in court or in mixed company – where it seems that a woman has **flesh,** or **genitals, genitalia, pudenda, femininity, privities, privates, private parts, womanhood, softness, eroticon** or **core of her being,** or what were presumably originally pet names such as her **tuzzy-muzzy** (also **tuzzi-muzzi), fan** (short for **fanny** – probably the commonest semi-polite term for the **tenuc** [backslang] in the UK. In the USA this word more commonly refers to the posteriors), **moniche, pussy** or **chat** (which is a French pussy).

Of course a lot of the fun of sexual activity lies in its forbidden nature. Pornography is always most sought after where it is least permitted. This is often brought up in some of the names given to the vulva. It was probable that they were first used by clergymen or parents working to instil their (public) ideas of correct behaviour for the distaff side, but they were soon adopted by the 'morts' and 'flash culls' (eighteenth and nineteenth century fast women and their male companions), at first in jest but later as everyday terms. Examples occur in such phrases as **putting the Devil into Hell** (= intromission), **party** (or **parts) of shame, fie for shame, the nameless, the name-it-not, the naughty and dirty work at the crossroads,** but these latter overlap with the more literary euphemisms. Examples here include the **flower of chivalry, End of the Sentimental Journey** (by Laurence Sterne: 'I put out my hand and caught hold of the fille-de-chambre's – '), **nest in the bush, where I live, mother of all souls, Love's pavilion, little sister, Love Lane, thing** (like the rabbit who had washed his thing and could not do a hare with it – thing is male or female), **affair, little woman, front door** (**front doormat** = pubic hair – because they always say Welcome), **agreeablements of life** and **eternal vale of men's delight.**

We can trace many pre-Freudian references to a partly

disguised fear of womankind (the *vagina dentata*) and of the gentle sex in general in such words and phrases as **vir gin** = man trap, **Fool's trap, Venus' Fly Trap, suck and swallow, fly cage, mousetrap** (where you put the mouse into the mousehole), **cat** (that catches the mouse – *see* the song *Ring Dang Doo*), **mangle,** etc. Contrariwise, its pleasure-giving propensities are extolled in **portal to the bower of bliss, welcome-mat** (= door-mat), **Gates of Paradise, mine of pleasure, lather-maker** and **hole of content.**

If we may withdraw from the vagina a moment, we can consider the terms used for the **hymen,** which was recently apotheosed as 'redundant in this permissive society' (wasn't it always?). They emphasize its inherent uselessness (**useless tissue**) or its fragility (real or supposed) and one-time-only nature – eg **tea-cup, Dame Nature's Privy Seal, pitcher** – or seriatim to the loss of blood traditionally attendant upon its passing (both meanings intended), eg **cherry.**

In due course (and the experienced anthropologist Jacobus X recommends that the husband should not, due to novelty and over-enthusiasm, accustom his bride during the honeymoon to a regime of such frequency of sexual embraces as he cannot thereafter keep up) the depucellated virgin is so **liquorish** that she could boast of a **much-travelled highway,** but this too easily becomes one that is slack and distended from too frequent childbearing, and she becomes worthy of the denominations **cow-cunted, bushel-cunted, sluice-cunted, double-cunted** or perhaps as **having a Main Street** or **Broadway.** The distressing effects (to those without a sense of humour. I knew someone who boasted of this ability) of the farting noises produced in the ploughing of such a furrow were described by TH van de Velde in his *Ideal Marriage*, and the famous *Bijou Cabinet* tells of the cunts that talked.

Despite the work of Freud, Ellis, and Masters and Johnson in pointing out the importance of diddling the clitoris or titillating the labia minora, the low vocabulary contains comparatively few terms for these parts. The common man is apparently still ignorant of the basic mechanisms involved in bringing off a woman, and still believes in an exclusively vaginal orgasm.

Some terms that have survived this ignorance include **little man in the boat** (or **boy in the boat**), **little ploughman**, **laborator naturae** (Rabelais), **little shame tongue** (a direct translation of the German) for *clitoris*, and **portals of sex, garden gate, gate in the orchard, cockles, double-sucker, ear between the legs, cat's head cut open,** etc, for the *lesser lips*. The *outer lips* are referred to as the **columns of Venus** – obviously a very old term, recalling the twin pillars of the portico of a temple dedicated to the goddess of love.

The anatomical relationship of the **bower of bliss** and its main channel is indicated in such phrases as the **front gut, foregut, forewoman, gape over the garter, lower mouth, the upright grin** (except, traditionally, in China), **a bit on a fork, The Great Divide** (occurs in the well-known poem 'Eskimo Nell'. It also refers to the cleavage 'an Australian use from the mountain range', especially a neckline of the Biblical type – **Lo and behold** – when her **dumplings are boiling over**), **hoop, leading article, dead end street** and **house under the hill**. The hill is the **mons pubis** (which is Latin for 'Fanny Hill'), but **dead end street** does not necessarily mean a cul-de-sac, but is more often used to imply that she is frigid. The English version is that he says, 'I'm sorry. I thought you moved.' The American goes, 'Let's fuck.' – 'Over my dead body.' – 'Of course. Why should tonight be any different?' The Australian is more earthy – 'D'you want a fuck?'– 'Like bloody hell.' – 'Well, d'you mind if I have one?'

Addresses more specific than these are more often found as graffiti in places where the paper is found in a roll than where it is bound in a book. Common examples include **Cockshire, Cock Inn, Cupid's Alley, Hairyfordshire, Crown and Feathers, Shooter's Hill, Mount Pleasant, Love Lane,** etc. The commonest lavatorial inscription used to be a mysterious message asking one to get in touch with *Miss Lucy Keeps, The Cockwell Inn, Tillit, Herts.* Perhaps I patronize a better-class bog nowadays, but I have not seen this for years. The elliptic mood is still sometimes found, however, in the advertisements of those on the game, where they delicately refer to *Miss Brown*, *Madam Brown*, *Itching Jenny*, *Mary Lane*, *Madge Howlett* and *Miss Laycock* in shop-window come-ons.

The abundance of words for the female pubic hair is not surprising when we consider that, unless she had an incipient Hottentot apron, the only part visible from the front or from the side when a woman stands or lies with her legs not unduly abducted, is the thatch overlying the Mount of Venus. It is interesting to compare the habits in such countries as Sweden, where the **nether beard** is often shaved yet it is considered sexy to leave the armpits hairy, with, say, Spain, where both parts are left in a state of nature. In India, both were once shaved (using a special ring called *ârsi*) but now both Moslems and Hindus use orpiment to produce smooth pubes (**shiny 'uns**) and smooth armpits. In the British Isles, it was regarded as worthy of a two-page spread in the *Daily Mirror* when Mary Quant said that she and her husband shave their pubic hair. Admittedly, additional interest was given by the fact that they shaved them to a heart shape, but why not, for heaven's sake? Nevertheless, very few women in this country shave **down below**, yet most shave their armpits. (Apart from some recent acquaintances, who wear no knickers of any kind, shave their fannies and wear rings and studs in their labia, the only women I have met who shave their pubic hairs are doctors' wives. I exclude those who do it for medical reasons.) Anyway, I think it is a pity. The shaving of armpits I blame on the rise of the United States as a leader of fashion, for there they believe that the sexual attraction of skin, sweat, hair (German proverb: Where there is hair there is pleasure), etc, should be drowned in a sea of deodorants, antiperspirants, scented soaps and shampoos. *O tempora! O mores!* The work of Kano (a Japanese: a people traditionally supposed to be obsessively cleanly) on the aphrodisiac properties of sweat appears to have been forgotten during the last twenty-five years. Any pheromones exuded on to the skin of the modern Miss (or Mrs) are stifled at birth, yet a small fortune is spent on replacing these natural beauty products with supposedly irresistible scents and perfumes. Let us remember that one of the earliest signs that the human female is becoming sexually receptive is the development of a generalised erythema, accompanied by a light exudation of sweat. So far as I know, this is identical in chemical composition with that produced by physical activity, though it would not be surprising if it were to differ, for there are many references in the literature to the different smell produced by the sweat of fear. This point would probably be well worthwhile investigating.

To leave the hirci (armpit hairs) and return to the **quim whiskers,** common terms include the geographical (**Bushey Park**), the botanical (**furzebush, forest, bush** and **parsley**), the nostalgic (**thatch.** It is said that a priest, walking through the wood, came across a girl, asleep, showing all she'd got. He covered her crotch with a tile that happened to be handy and walked on. A little later two old men wandered by. One looked long, then turned to the other, saying, 'In my day they were covered with thatch.'), the derisive (**fur, fluff**) and the punning (**furbelow, muff** [definition: a soft furry thing that keeps the hand warm without squeezing it], and **front-door mat**). Sometimes it is referred to as a **malkin** or **merkin,** which is properly a **quim-wig,** used when everyone slept naked and a common effect of smallpox was the loss of the pubic hair. I have heard that these are making a comeback in Sweden, though I have traced none in my visits there. The purpose now is simply variety. **Quim-bush** is not often used, nowadays.

There is a small family of names for the **snatch-thatch** based upon the tax imposed on English playing cards in the days of Queen Anne. Because no one likes paying *any* tax, this was regarded as a devilish device to reap benefit from the Devil's picture book and the ornate tax device on the ace of spades was given jocular nicknames in reference to the Prince of Hell. It being well known that this card resembles the female escutcheon, the latter became known as **Old Frizzle, Frizzle,** and the **ace of spades,** which reminds us of the young lady who nearly won the fancy dress contest. She turned up wearing only black gloves and black boots, as the five of spades, but was beaten by the ace of hearts.

# THE MALE ORGAN OF INTROMISSION

The anatomical term for this organ is the *penis*. This comes from the Latin for 'pencil'. In fact, in Latin, the two terms were to a certain extent interchangeable, though the writing implement differed from our modern pencils. This inter-changeability of the terms is not generally known, so that I have been known to stop all conversation in a crowded room by announcing, 'I have a gold-plated, self-propelling penis.' The similarity between the penis and the modern writing implement – the ball-point pen – has not escaped the attention of the advertising world. There were current until recently advertisements in all national dailies for a certain brand of ball-pen. This showed a greatly enlarged view of the ball (itself an evocative term) which at first glance looked more like a penis, with the prepuce partly retracted to expose most of the glans. I do not know the effect on sales, but this advertisement appeared unchanged as to the illustration (I never read the words) for eighteen months.

In modern English, however, these stationery terms have survived only at the extremes of the span of human life. The little boy's external genitalia are referred to as his **pencil** and **tassel**, and the **old man**, when, alas, **free of Fumblers' Hall**, is said to have **no more ink in the pen** or **no more lead in the pencil**.

Nevertheless, **old man** can mean the **Moby Dick** itself, and **the old man has got his Sunday clothes on** (which were starched) means the part is erect. It is less certain whether the old man is able only to gam her in phrases like **to give the old man his supper** (= to receive a man sexually) or **to warm the old man's supper**, which is to sit with the skirts raised before the fire. It may mean 'old man' as simply the regular sexual partner or it may mean he can only **eat** her (ie **go muff-diving**, or **muff-noshing**) – and the only way she can supple both ends of it (ie remove its starch) is **to suck his sugar-stick**.

Long before Freud was even a gleam in his father's eye, the ingenuity of the common man (who is much more common in both senses than one would suspect from a study of the legal assumptions as to his actions and understanding) had applied the name of practically every outstanding feature to the male organ – eg **obelisk, column, monument, rod, pole, yard, halbert, drumstick, bilbo,** etc. Freud merely reversed the process and called all these objects 'phallic symbols'.

Some of these words may seem presumptuous to the normally endowed man (one who is neither 'short and thick, like a Welshman's prick' nor donged like a donkey), but it must be borne in mind that it is the erectness, strength, rigidity and upstanding that is being adopted. **Yard** refers not to the imperial measure of length directly, but to the **arrow** (**verge, flèche, bolt, dart, Cupid's dart**), which was for many years the standard male weapon everywhere.

The reverse process of this abstraction or depersonification of the penis is its personification, either impersonally as **little man, foreman, him,** or personally as **Dick, John Thomas, JT , John Willie, man Thomas,** etc.

The term **Jack** is not really a name of this sort. Like many of these terms, it has multiple meanings and multiple shades of meanings. A *jack* was an inferior man; it is a device for lifting things (eg an erection); it was a roasting spit, and **to roast** is to copulate with; it is related to the donkey (**donkey dick** = rhyming slang on *prick*) via jackass; jack screws are big ones, and screwing is **having it off; to play Irish whist** is when the Jack takes the Ace (= **Old Frizzle**); and Jack is a variant of Jock (the crutch) and Jacob, so that **to get Jack into the orchard** is to penetrate her; *Jacob's ladder* leads to Heaven; and of course **to leap up a ladder** is for intimacy to take place.

**Dick** is also complex. It is supposed to be a contraction of Derrick, the famous hangman of the days of the first Elizabeth who was so skillful at turning them off that his name became generally adopted for a lifting device. In the oil fields of Texas, the derrick is a tall, erect machine, gushing forth if one is lucky, but **dick** or **dickie** ('a false front') is also short for **dickory-dock** (rhyming slang on *cock*) and for **donkey dick**, which is a well-known undoubtedly male animal, well-hung or well-endowed with family jewels. That is, its **muscle** is prominent – so-called because it works better after exercise and always feels better after a good rub-down.

Compared with the terms for the female external organs of generation, few of the common terms for the **tool** are euphemisms. This may be because men usually refer to their parts in no uncertain terms, as **cock, jock, prick, tool, root,** or in the grandiose, boastful style of **pikestaff, bone, coupling bat,** etc. It is only in a court of law, or, sometimes when conversing with a doctor, that such terms as **private parts, privates** or **my organ** may be heard. (It was in court that a woman was asked by counsel 'if he had introduced his organ?' – 'It was more like a flute, your honour,' she replied.) Women sometimes use such terms as **maleness, manhood,** or **himself,** and the seeming diminutives of **needle, bodkin, core** and **cory** (from the Romany *kori* = a needle) were probably originally euphemisms for *prick*. When Angus Ogilvy married Princess Alexandra, I heard a woman on a Sheffield bus say to her neighbour, 'Well, I suppose he'll be tossing his **caber** tonight.'

Polite words for children occur, such as **doodle,** but this is related to *cock* via **cock-a-doodle-doo;** and a **doodle-dandler** is one who **flogs the bishop,** ie **wanks off. Flap-doodle, doodle-flap, flapper,** and **floater** may refer to a young boy or to an old man, the one never having experienced a cock-stand and the other a matter of memory. In the same way, **tiddler** means not only a little boy's whistle but that which is used to tiddle with, but **diddler** is the first or that which is used **to diddle** (= titillate) the **diddley-pout** = vagina.

The use of euphemisms, circumlocution and elegant variation is roundly and soundly condemned by Eric Partridge in his *Usage and Abusage,* yet other authorities praise John Cleland for the way his *Fanny Hill* contains no 'rude' words and they condemn the supposed monotony of 'cheap' pornography. As will be seen, the phrases used in *Fanny Hill* are, in intent at least, as 'rude' as any of the commoner terms, which have the advantage of brevity and unambiguity. Pornography is not cheap and, for example, in the Olympia Press edition of *Lucrezia Borgia, Part 1,* I came across thirty-three terms for the male and female sexual parts that I had not until then come across. This is considerably more than the *total* number of terms used by Cleland in *Fanny Hill* for the same organs. I found him very monotonous with his 'avenue of pleasure', 'main avenue', etc. Admittedly, that part of Miss Hill was well travelled and there was much 'dirty work at the crossroads', but within limits, I prefer variety. Compare this paragraph from 'Sub-Umbra or Sport among the She-Noodles', in *The Pearl* (Vol. I No. 1 [July 1879]; Grove Press reprint of 1968):

> 'Ah, coz dear, can you be so innocent? Feel here the dart of love all impatient to enter the mossy grotto between your thighs,' I whispered, placing her hand upon my prick, which I had suddenly let out of the restraining trousers. 'How you sigh; grasp it in your hand, dear, is it possible that you do not understand what it is for?'
>
> Her face was crimson to the roots of her hair, as her hand grasped my tool, and her eyes seemed to start with terror at the sudden apparition of Mr John Thomas; so that taking advantage of her speechless confusion my own hand, slipping under her clothes, soon had possession of her mount, and in spite of the nervous contraction of her thighs, the forefinger searched out the virgin clitoris.

The anonymous author could certainly teach Cleland a thing or two about elegant variation, though he himself needs schooling in elementary punctuation. Note also the way the narrator uses poetic phrases such as 'dart of love' when addressing the coy maiden, but supposes the reader is more sophisticated, so that he uses the simpler, cruder, terms 'prick' and 'tool' and the jocular 'Mr John Thomas' when addressing him.

Sometimes in such works the organ is referred to in diminuendo fashion. This is not really belittling: you are not supposed to take it literally. It is more in the nature of mock modesty, with a presumption that there is a lot to be modest about. Examples are **mouse, carrot** or **bodkin,** though the **bodkin** is usually the largest needle in the pack (it is also used as a technical term for a pin stuck into or through the hair); still it is smaller than a **broadsword** or a **pikestaff**. Of course, these words overlap with the previous section – those names derived from the slang terms for the female parts. Thus the **mouse** goes into the **mousehole,** the **carrot** is used to tempt the

**cunny-warren**, the **kennel-raker** rakes the **kennel**, the **kennedy** (= poker) pokes the **fires of Hell**, the **wedge** enters the **crack** and the **placket-racket** engages with the **placket**.

Sometimes specialized tools and implements are brought in. Thus, who, after learning that the correct technicality for a **shunter's pole** is a **coupling bat**, could resist applying either term to the pole used for a different kind of coupling? Similar puns occur with the terms **joy-stick** and **dipstick** – I overheard in a cinema once the cry 'Keep your lipstick off my dipstick!'

Sometimes this process is combined with a reference to **come-juice** and **coming** – eg **shooting stick** or **shooting iron**, **culty gun**, **cream-stick**, **cremorne** = **cream horn**. Sometimes the process is more complicated, and we have the double inversion seen in the use of **shunter's pole** for *prick* with eg **torrac** = **carrot** (= Spanish *garrote* = stick). Single inversion is seen in back-slang, eg **enob**, and to a certain extent in rhyming slang, where the elision of the rhymed word is common. For example, **Colleen** = **Colleen Bawn** (= rhyming slang on *horn*), as is **Marquess** = **Marquess of Lorne**, and we have seen already **donkey** = **donkey dick** (= rhyming slang on *prick*). The elision of the other word is less common, but it does occur, as in **wick** = **Hampton wick** (= rhyming slang on *prick*), though **Hampton** is also commonly used by itself. Elision also occurs with **bean**, which is short for **beanstalk** or **beanpole**.

We also come across specialized terms in the male mastur-bation phrases such as **flog the bishop**, **gallop one's antelope**, **jerk one's mutton**, **pull one's wire** (or **pud**), **shake hands with the bloke who enlisted with one** or **do a doodle-dandler**. More restricted uses are met in the catch questions, 'Do you like rhubarb and custard?' and 'Do you like bananas and cream?' **Melted butter** is **spunk**. There is a common saying, 'She looked as though butter wouldn't melt in her mouth, but . . . ' **To melt** is the same as **to meld**, **to have a merry bout**, **to sleep with**, **swive with**, **copulate with**, **lay**, **screw**, **serve**, **mate with**, **enjoy**, **make love to** or **with**, **to lie together**, **to be united**, **to sleep together** ('Did you sleep with this woman?' – 'Not a wink, your honour'), **to have it off**, **up** or **away**. In other words, intimacy, or sexual relations, took place.

The greengrocery words associated with the penis are of four main classes. First, there are those that are merely familiarizing less well known words. The prime example of this has been given above, **carrot** for **garrote** = stick (?rhyming slang on *prick*). Second, we have those terms taken from folklore – eg **haricot** = French for **bean** = short for **beanstalk**, which is familiar to us all from the nursery and pantomime. If planted aright, it grows *ever* so tall. **Gooseberries** for the testicles is of the same group, for traditionally little girls are found in the *parsley bed* (= female escutcheon), whereas little boys come from under the *gooseberry bush*. The third and most numerous group of fruit and vegetable synonyms comes from analogy with the corresponding feminine terms, so that the **gardener tends the garden** or **cabbage patch**. **Fig** is used here, but it can also refer to the vulva, as is seen in Aristophanes' *The Peace*:

> Now live splendidly together,
> Free from adversity.
> Pick your figs.
> May his be large and hard.
> May hers be sweet.

– and this usage has persisted through the years so that the *fica* remains a common Italian gesture of concupiscence or contempt.

The fourth compartment contains those words already discussed as of limited usage – **bananas** and **rhubarb**.

These are not the only edible terms, however. The grocery, the butcher's and the sweet shop are all represented as well as the greengrocer's. Thus there is **almond** (**-rock** = rhyming slang on *cock*), **cracker** (goes off like a firework), **banger** (a sausage, so-called because it spits when put in the **oven** = **chuff-box**), **sausage, haulkin** (= a large sausage), **taddler** (another large sausage), **wiener** and **hot dog, pud, pudding** (older terms for sausage), **meat, gristle, bone, sugar-stick** and **cremorne**. Although **hot dog** is more commonly used in the United States literature, presumably from the likeness, real or imagined, the sausage terms have largely fallen from use, although one still hears **black pudding** for a black man's organ. In Britain, a butcher's wife was granted a divorce from her husband, on the ground of mental cruelty ('Does he beat you?' – 'Yes. Every time he beats me.'). Finding him less lusty than suited her temperament, she brought herself off each night with black puddings from the shop. She washed them before returning them to the shop for sale, she said.

Then there is the jargon of instrumental use – either analogous or punning. These include the specialized terms from railway life, such as **coupling bat** and **lollipop** ('a shafted tool, with an iron ball, used for disturbing sleepers') and from the orchestra, such as **fiddling stick, fiddle bow, fiddle stick, drum-stick** (used for beating the drum), **organ** and **flute** and even **trombone** (from the in-and-out action). We also find the policeman represented with his **truncheon, billie, night stick** or **copper stick** (which is also a housewife's tool of the last century) and the engineer with his **derrick, screwdriver, rogering iron, piston** and **pumphandle.** Weaponry is particularly well represented whether for length (**pikestaff**), as gun (**culty gun** or **shooting iron**), as edged tool (**culty gun** again, for culty = Latin *culter* = knife; **sword, blade, broadsword, blade, bilbo, fox, falchion,** etc) or as a blunt instrument (**cudgel, club, crozier** or **doob** – an Australian aboriginal word for a pipe of hollow wood). A pointed weapon may be involved, such as a **pike, prong, pronger, harpoon** or **Colleen** (**Bawn** = rhyming slang on *horn*).

Pathological conditions and normal variants are fairly well represented, so that a man who has chordee (a painful bent condition of the penis) is said to have penile strabismus, or its literal translation, 'squint of the cock' – or he may be said to be **hock-pintled** or **hock-pointed** or **to have a lobcock** – though one should not confuse this use of **hock** with a *hock* as an associate with *poufters*, for this means he is **as queer as a two-quid note** or **a three-speed walking stick.** A man without testes is referred to as a **rascal** (from the deer), and if he is **ricked**, he is said **to be added to the list** (of steeplechasers in training).

A **dropping member** is a penis that may be erect or flaccid, especially when it is afflicted with the clap. The difference between the flaccid and the turgid part is best exemplified by the tale of **Dr Johnson** (another term for the penis, by the way. Partridge says, 'Perhaps because there was no one he was not prepared to stand up to,' though this phrase may have been an unfortunate choice as it implies unchastity at least and possibly immorality): he is alleged to have been seen in a 'tay house' (teahouse) **showing an Abyssinian medal,** ie with his flies undone. 'Sir,' said a woman, 'your penis is sticking out.' 'Madam,' said the Great Cham, 'you flatter yourself. My penis is hanging out.'

A **stand** or a **hard-on** is an erection or **stargazer,** which can also be a **hedge-whore** – that is **one who goes stargazing on her back** and **receives an Anglo-Indian back.** In other words, she has **done a rural.** The erect organ is specifically indicated in **hard bit, hard mouthful, hard-on** and **hard-up,** and the flaccid part is referred to as **Hanging Johnny, doodle-flap** and **flapper.**

After swimming, one may still hear the expression **I'm so cold I don't know if I'm Agnes or Angus** (or **Arthur or Martha,** as they put it in Australia). This refers to the cremasteric reflex – the physiological retraction of the scrotum, with elevation of the testes, on exposure to cold or on tickling the inside of the upper thigh. Apropos of this, an epidemic swept through Singapore and Malaysia a few years ago. This was the disease called *koro,* which crops up again and again over the years in the Chinese population. They become convinced that the penis is growing smaller and is retracting into the body so that eventually it would disappear altogether.


## TESTICULAR TERMS AND SEMINAL SYNONYMS

As with the mainstem, it is not usual for the testes to be belittled, even in a jocular fashion, as to their size or function. Indeed, the old story illustrating what is meant by the psychiatric term 'delusions of grandeur' is very apt. A man is said to have attended the pox doctor's clinic complaining that one ball had swollen to the size of a football – and the other had shrunk to the size of a grapefruit.

*Testicle* is not really a diminutive of *testis,* because it means 'a little witness' (to a man's virility), so that reference to one's testimonials is not catachrestic or malapropery. In fact, it is etymologically correct, even if anatomically untrue, to refer to one's testicles as **monsters,** for **monster** comes from the Latin *monstro* = I show, or in other words, 'that which demonstrates something'.

For these reasons these organs ('Two is a luxury') are commonly called **balls** or **ballocks, stones** or **dusters, apples** or **nuts.** The precise nuts are rarely indicated, but they vary from **coconuts** (in the West Indian calypso *Marianne*) to **nutmegs,** which, if it is the size that is being compared, would be slightly smaller than average. Perhaps it is the hardness that is meant, though that, if literal, would indicate severe disease. The apparent diminutive of **pills** disappears when it is realized that it is the Latin *pila* that is meant, ie 'ball'.

Rhyming slang has many terms for these **berries** and we hear 'He hit me in the **orchestra**' = **orchestra stalls** = **balls,** or **coffee** = **coffee stalls,** or **cobblers** (often assumed to be thus, as an exclamation, but properly **cobbler's**) = **cobbler's awls** (= rhyming slang on *balls*). **Beecham's (pills)** as rhyming slang on **testikills**(!) and **flowers** (**and frolics**) or **fun and frolics** as rhyming slang on **bollicks** are rarer.

Terms such as **nags** and **marbles,** or **pounders,** or **ladies' jewels, tarriwags** or **knackers** all refer to the same thing. The last also means a horse-slaughterer and are a sort of medieval bongo drumset!

The scrotum that contains the **nuts** is rarely mentioned. **Ball bag** and **bag** are uncommon terms in themselves, though the last survives in the phrase **last shake of the bag,** meaning 'one's youngest child'.

In contrast there are many terms for the ejaculate that is the end result of your **chuff and chutty: cream, letchwater, lewd infusion, living injection, fetch, fuck, melted butter, honey, spunk** and **lather** are all fairly common terms, and when the **red-hot poker** is **foaming at the mouth** and **ready to spit,** the **gasp and grunt** (rhyming slang) should be ready to let down its **spendings.**

# UP, UP AND AWAY

(Popular song, 1969)

The terms used for copulating and the sexual act are in one sense unimaginative, because they very largely consist of variations on the theme of vague ideas such as **have it off, up** or **away**. These are not really euphemistic because it is implicit that no ambiguity could possibly result and, unlike euphemisms, they are, or used to be, avoided in polite, mixed company. Related to this group are the allusive **up her petticoats, up her way, play at up-tails-all, make the beast with two backs** (*Othello*), **go tummy-tickling, play rub-belly, match ends, get up, to take a turn among the cabbages, among her frills, in Abraham's bosom, on Shooter's Hill, in Hair Court, among the parsley** or **through the stubble**. There are also the vague **do jig-a-jig** and **play hanky-panky**.

There are various semi-technical terms for acting thus, such as **grind, screw, twang, shag, fuck, swive, roger, copulate, coit, flute** and **go tromboning**. Those derived from the words for the penis or vulva include **to take Nebuchadnezzar out to grass**, where **grass** = **greens** (from Priapus as a garden god as well as a phallic deity), **to trot out one's pussy** or the various ones and others quoted at **take a turn** above. It should be noted that all except one of these phrases refer to the male and his performance, but the ladies are not neglected. When Eblis has caused a moisture to flow, the vulva can **get her wheel greased**, when she is said **to have fed her pussy, having gone all the way** or **the limit**. She is a **Lady Hotbot**, who **likes her oats, greens** or her **grommet**. A **roundheels** like this is in such a state that the least push sends her **on her back**.

On the other hand, she may **go off the boil** and may then **employ the freeze** to get what she wants. Or she may permit **a bit of bazooka** (= all but), refraining from sexual intercourse because **the flag is up**, indicating that **the captain** (or **cardinal**) **is home**. Of course, liquorice-all-sorts would not let this stop them from **having their lamp lit** (Radclyffe Hall, *The Unlit Lamp*).

If, though, she should be afraid of **getting clucky** and **falling to pieces**, she may be satisfied with **French kissing, French tricks** or **a flying 66** (rhyming slang on *French tricks*), though this practice may best be seen amongst lesbians or others who prefer **soixante-neuf** to a **flat fuck** (**soixante-neuf** is **mutual growl-biting**). Alternatively, she may like **to play hot cockles** or allow someone else **to fumble, feel** or **finger-fuck** her. Girls go wild over **finger pie**.

Still, when she meets a **whisker-splitter**, a **mort wap-apace** usually prefers to be **fettled** properly – even as a **floor-fuck** or by **doing a perpendicular** (which is a **knee-trembler**), though we would all agree that the best place **to make feet for childrens' shoes** is on the device for manufacturing motors for tricycles and providing he is wearing a **Jo-bag** she should not be **storked**. (In plain English: 'When she meets a man well known for his success with the ladies, a woman with a liking for sexual intercourse usually prefers the conventional penis-vagina contact [compared with the deep-petting, cunnilingus, manustupration, etc, of the previous paragraph], though we would all agree that the most comfortable place for that action that is likely to result in pregnancy is on the bed, but if he is wearing a condom, then she should escape impregnation, with any luck.')

The different positions that may be assumed for more or less satisfactory mutual pleasuring are included in the low vocabulary. The semi-technical terms of *The Perfumed Garden* and of the *Kama Sutra* – the Congress of the Cow, The Lotus Tree, etc – have no established technical terms in English. Until the mass production of cheap editions recently, only the erudite scholar knew of these **filthy tricks**.

Our people have stuck to the **missionary position**, so called from those well-meaning souls who believed that any way other than man on top, woman beneath, supine ('stargazing on one's back') was indecent and immoral. The usual position in Oceania was with the man squatting between the woman's abducted legs, rocking backwards and forwards on his heels. We have no name for this.

Should the man remain superior, but the woman turn prone,

he is said **to rump** her. If she brings her legs up to raise her **bimbo** so she is in the knee-chest or knee-elbow position, they are said to be doing it **dog-fashion** or **dog-style**. Were they to roll on to their sides, our coupling couple would be doing it **Chinese fashion**. If she assumes the superior position, they are said to be **riding rantipole**, with **the dragon on Saint George** – a position which is said to favour the begetting of bishops.

If he is not particular as to whether he gets her **'twixt wind and water**, he may prefer **to shoot her in the tail, to rim** or **bottle** her, ie **to get stuck into her Rory Douglas** – that part which has one eye and a stinking breath. On the other hand, they may indulge in a **69**, with reciprocal **muff-noshing** and **knob-gobbling**, if they are both **linguists**.

In any case, we would all agree that **a push in the bush** is worth two in the hand, that is, that **to pump one's pickle** or **jerk one's gherkin** (Canadian terms, these) is not so satisfactory as **to lay a wench**. Of course, one might meet a **prick-teaser** (**p.t.**) who refuses a present for a good girl ('Mother told me to be good. Was I?'), so one may have to resort to the **Portuguese pump** willy-nilly, no matter how much one would wish **to polish one's arse on the top sheet**.


## IN AN INTERESTING CONDITION: HEAVY WITH CHILD

Phrases regarding the expectant state fall into three main groups – the euphemistic, the phrases suggesting misfortune and those suggesting she has struck lucky.

In the first, most numerous, class, we have **clucky, broody, she is not alone, in an interesting condition, in a certain state** or **condition, with a kid in the basket, up the duff = in the club = in the pudden** or **pudding club, coming, up the spout, preggers, in the family** or **familial way, carrying all before her, eating for two, in a delicate state of health** or **carrying the bass drum**.

In the second class, one encounters such phrases as **been sitting in the garden with the garden gate unlocked** and **shot**

**in the tail.** Doubly unfortunate is she who has **Martin's hammer knocking at the wicket,** for she is expecting twins. **Gone** or **got into trouble** is specifically unmarried pregnancy, and **holed out in one** is pregnant after only one sexual act. After all, it is said that larks in the night are responsible for more births than are storks.

The more pleased terms for pregnancy include **clicked, expectant, anticipating** and **expecting a happy event.** Slanguage assumes that children are unfortunate accidents, or, as Oliver Anderson puts it, 'a perpetual reminder of a pardonable error in the heat of the moment'. This seems to be a reference to **getting off at Redfern,** which is an Australian term, for Redfern is the last station before Sydney Central, so this is used for *coitus interruptus.*

The future father may be praised, saying he has her **sewn up** or **tied up,** which means he has impregnated her and has nothing to do with infibulation or kinky bondage games.

There are a few terms for being brought to childbed, such as **come to grief** or **fall to pieces,** and even the condition afterwards is thought of as **bushel-cunted** and **wrinkle-bellied.** Her breasts may droop from **knockers** or **thrusters** to **dingle-danglers** or, worse, **spaniel's ears.**

The end-product of all this activity, the baby ('a spoonful of modified snot in the womb', as the Marquis de Sade put it so nicely) may be **one nick** or **two nick** – printer's terms for 'baby boy' and 'baby girl' respectively: they are also referred to as **certainty** and **uncertainty.** A **chance-child** is one that has been **born on the wrong side of the blanket,** ie a bastard.

If perchance she should abort, she is said to have **slipped her calf** or **cast the wanes.** Traditionally gin (mother's ruin) is the best abortifacient drug, but a **chimney-sweeper** (black draught), an aperient, may be equally effective.

Earlier stages of prevention are characterized by various contraceptive devices. The condom is known as a **skin, frogskin, French letter** or **Jo-bag.** For once the French do not take all the credit or blame and the **vault cap** or diaphragm is known as the **Dutch cap,** whereas the cervical cap, so beloved of Marie Stopes, is called the **capot anglais,** 'English raincoat'. One brand of quinine pessary was called the **Mother's Friend,** but to the user it was known as the **Midwife's Friend,** from its unreliability.

The pill was unknown in the days of my major research and even now it has not acquired a nickname, except that the pill is catachrestic, for all on the market are tablets, not pills. It is said that the best oral contraceptive is the word 'No', but others prefer a Polo mint clasped firmly between the knees. American readers may need to be informed that Polo mints are like Lifesavers. The big rival mint in Britain is the Trebor mint, which has no orifice, so is known to some as the 'virgin Polo'. In the old days they were advised to take orange juice – 'Before or after?' – 'Instead.'

Enough has been said here to enable the **cherry prick** (a cock virgin) to hold his own (or not to be left holding his own) in any **trugging ken** (a house of ill repute). He can understand the talk around him, he can tell what is on offer and, if all else fails, he can always state his requirements in plain English. A study of these terms should help make his English even plainer, and we might get more imaginative pornography.

---

## SHAKESPEARE'S OPINION

. . . to gain the language,
'T is needful that the most immodest word
Be look'd upon and learn'd . . .

*King Henry IV*, Part II, 4.4.69–71

# THE OFFICIAL NEW MAN'S SEX QUIZ

Study each statement carefully, then write **T** for *true* or **F** for *false* after each item.

1. A **clitoris** is a type of flower.
2. A **pubic hair** is a wild rabbit.
3. A **vulva** is an automobile from Sweden.
4. **Spread eagle** refers to an extinct bird.
5. A **fallopian tube** is a part of a television set.
6. It is dangerous to have a **wet dream** under an electric blanket.
7. McDonald's 'Golden Arches' are a **phallic symbol**.
8. **Vagina** is a medical term to describe heart trouble.
9. A **fellatio** is an Italian dagger.
10. A **menstrual cycle** has three wheels.
11. A **G-string** is part of a violin.
12. **Semen** is another term for sailors.
13. **Anus** is the Latin word for 'year'.
14. **Testicles** are found on an octopus.
15. A **cunnilingus** is a person who can speak four languages.
16. **Asphalt** is a medical term to describe rectal problems.
17. **Feminine Freshness** is when a girl asks you out on a date.
18. **Masturbate** is something needed to catch large fish.
19. **Coitus** is a musical instrument.
20. **Foetus** is a character on *Gunsmoke*.
21. An **umbilical cord** is part of a parachute.
22. A **condom** is a large apartment complex.
23. An **orgasm** is the person who accompanies the church choir.
24. A **diaphragm** is a drawing in geometry.

25. A **dildo** is a variety of sweet pickle.
26. An **erection** is held when the Japanese vote.
27. A **lesbian** is a person from the Middle East.
28. **Sodomy** is a special kind of fast-growing grass.
29. **Pornography** is the business of making records.
30. **Genitals** are people of non-Jewish origin.
31. **Douche** is the French word for 'twelve'.
32. An **enema** is someone who is not your friend.
33. **Ovaries** is a French egg dish made with cheese.
34. **Scrotum** is a small planet next to Uranus.
35. **Phallus** is a city on the Nile.
36. **Cunt** was a famous German philosopher.
37. **Twat** is an interrogative pronoun.
38. **VD** is a bank holiday celebrated on 11 November.
39. **Herpes** was a Greek king.
40. **Incests** are studied by entomologists.
41. The **ben-wa ball** is held in Tokyo on 1 June.
42. A **pessary** is a wild pig.
43. **Copulation** is sex between two consenting policemen.
44. An **ovarian cyst** is an Armenian desert.
45. **Mutual Orgasm** is an insurance company.
46. A **homosexual** is a technician who purifies milk.
47. The **clap** is a reward you get for a fine performance.
48. **Tampax** is a city on the Florida coastline.
49. **Anilingus** is a movie star from India.
50. A **drag queen** is the winner in a hot-rod race.
51. An **IUD** is a promissory note.
52. A **sanitary belt** is a drink from a clean shot-glass.
53. A **rectum** is what you are for taking this quiz.

---

What's the difference between a dyke and a lesbian?
– *The dyke kick-starts her dildo.*

What's the definition of a *rugged* woman?
– *One who kick-starts her own vibrator and rolls her own tampons.*

# FOUR WAYS TO AVOID
# UNPLEASANTNESS

(George W S Trow)

ESCAPE the ugly consequences of Straightforward Speech

Learn EUPHEMISM
The Language of Evasion

---

*Do you need Euphemism?* Read these sentences:

1. You're a Jew, aren't you, Mary?
2. Thank God I'm rich.
3. I'd like to take you out, Alice, but frankly, I'm a homosexual.
4. So many people of your age seem to be dead.

---

Did you spot the treacherous Straightforward Words (evocative of painful *reality*) in these simple sample sentences? If you didn't, you can expect endless difficulty and embarrassment in your pathetic little life. Let's *review* the FIVE MOST TREACHEROUS WORDS IN OUR MOTHER TONGUE, the words that cry out for translation into Euphemism, the language of evasion. They are (and, if you play your cards right, you need never face them again): 'JEW', 'RICH', 'HOMOSEXUAL', 'DEAD', and 'FRANKLY'. Learn Euphemism, the only language endorsed by the Department of Health, Education, and Welfare (as well as three leading Midwestern universities), and we'll tell you how to avoid these dread words, EVEN WHEN TALKING TO OR ABOUT MARCEL PROUST!*

103

*Our booklet, 'The Lore of Euphemism', available for a nominal fee, tells the moving story of Euphemscholar Nancy Tmolin, who translated the sentence 'Frankly, Marcel, you're a rich, dead, homosexual Jew' into Euphemism in ten seconds flat.

## Now Look at the Subtle Problems Posed by this Second Group of Sample Sentences:

1. How come you don't have any children?
2. I have plenty of time, Mother, and I would come to see you more often, but actually I find you depressing.
3. I guess you're in the hospital for good this time.
4. How many toes do you have, anyway?

## We'll teach you to defuse even these problem sentences.

1. You will learn ten ways to discuss the Middle Eastern Situational Conflict without ever mentioning the ugly word 'Jew'.
2. You will discuss *without blushing* people who are no longer alive!
3. You will learn the language secrets of the Carolinas (North and South), where absolutely nothing is said!
4. You will wear the miracle Eu-pho-phone (yew-foe-foe-nn), which automatically bleeps out offensive words in the speech of others.

---

Why did God create gentiles?
– *Well*, somebody *has to pay retail*!

Why did Jesus cross the road?
– *Because He was nailed to a chicken.*

What do you call a nun with one leg?
– *Hopalong Chastity.*

# IMPURE MATHEMATICS

## (Anon)

Once upon a time (1/T) pretty little Polly Nomial was strolling across a field of vectors when she came to the edge of a singularly large matrix.

Now, Polly was convergent and her mother had made it an absolute condition that she must never enter such an array without her brackets on. Polly, however, who had changed her variables that morning and was feeling particularly badly behaved, ignored this condition on the grounds that it was insufficient and made her way in amongst the complex elements.

Rows and columns enveloped her on all sides. Tangents approached her surface. She became tensor and tensor. Quite suddenly, three branches of a hyperbola touched her at a single point. She oscillated violently, lost all sense of directrix and went completely divergent. As she reached a turning point she tripped over a square root which was protruding from the erf and plunged headlong down a steep gradient. When she was differentiated once more, she found herself, apparently alone, in a non-Euclidean space.

She was being watched, however. That smooth operator, Curly Pi, was lurking inner product. As his eyes devoured her curvilinear coordinates, a singular expression crossed his face. 'Was she still convergent?' he wondered. He decided to integrate improperly at once.

Hearing a vulgar fraction behind her, Polly turned around and saw Curly Pi approaching with his power series extrapolated. She could see at once, by his degenerate conic and his dessipative terms, that he was bent on no good.

'Eureka!' she gasped.

'Ho, ho,' he said. 'What a symmetric little Polynomial you are. I can see you're bubbling over with secs.'

'O Sir,' she protested, 'keep away from me. I haven't got my brackets on.'

105

'Calm yourself, my dear,' said our suave operator. 'Your fears are purely imaginary.'

'I . . . I,' she thought, 'perhaps he's homogeneous then.'

'What order are you?' the brute demanded.

'Seventeen,' replied Polly.

Curly leered. 'I suppose you've never been operated on yet?' he asked.

'Of course not,' Polly cried indignantly. 'I'm absolutely convergent.'

'Come, come,' said Curly. 'Let's go off to a decimal place I know, and I'll take you to the limit.'

'Never!' gasped Polly.

'Exchlf!' he swore, using the vilest oath he knew. His patience was gone. Coshing her over the coefficient with a log until she was powerless, Curly removed her discontinuities. He stared at her significant places and began smoothing her points of inflexion. Poor Polly. All was up. She felt his hand tending to her asymptotic limit. Her convergence would soon be gone forever.

There was no mercy, for Curly was a heavyside operator. He integrated by parts. He integrated by partial fractions. The complex beast even went all the way around and did a contour integration. What an indignity to be multiply-connected on her first integration! Curly went on operating until he was absolutely and completely orthogonal.

When Polly got home that evening, her mother noticed that she had been truncated in several places. But it was too late to differentiate now. As the months went by, Polly increased monotonically. Finally she generated a small but pathological function which left surds all over the place until she was driven to distraction.

The moral of our sad story is this: if you want to keep your expressions convergent, never allow them a single degree of freedom.

---

Why do they call camels the Ships of the Desert?
– *Because they are full of Arab seamen.*

Why did the Baptists outlaw fucking?
– *Because it might lead to dancing.*

# ΠΥΓΜΉ – ΦΑΛΛΌΣ
# FIST – PHALLUS

(Elias Petropoulos)

Two related gestures are used in modern Greece by way of insult: the fist-phallus and the finger-phallus. The finger-phallus gesture is known colloquially as *kōlodakhtylo* (literally, 'the finger for the ass'), which refers more to the action of 'goosing' than to the mere gesture. The slang expression, *Tha sou valō kōlodakhtylo* ('I will put the finger in your ass') means metaphorically: I will punish you, I will make things hard for you. The finger-phallus gesture is simple. To form or express it, one has only to bend the middle finger downward, while moving the hand up and down, *or* wiggling the finger at the same time (but not both the hand and finger together), and looking straight into the eyes of the person to whom the insulting gesture is directed. (See Figure 4.)

The finger-phallus (δάχτυλος–φαλλός) or *kōlodakhtylo* gesture has an impressive history, since it is known at least from the time of Socrates (5th century BC). The fist-phallus gesture (Πυγμη-φαλλος), which does not seem to have any popular name, is almost equally old. The German literary historian, Ernst Theodor Echtermeyer, in 1833, pointed out a passage

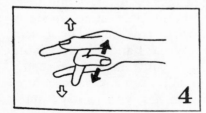
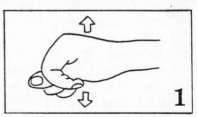

in the Latin poet Ovid (1st century BC) where the gesture of the fist-phallus is described, and eighty years later the Greek folklorist N Politis corroborated Echtermeyer's interpretation of Ovid, but without adding anything more on the subject. I will try to fill this gap here.

The fist-phallus gesture is very common in Greece, especially among members of the underworld. The gesture is performed by passing or thrusting the thumb between the index and middle fingers, and then pointing this phallic fist at the person to be insulted. Three variations of the fist-phallus gesture can be distinguished, according to the intensity of the insult intended.

**Variation No. I:** The insulter shows the fist-phallus and pushes it at the insulted person's snout, shaking the fist-phallus up and down four or five times. The fist is kept in horizontal position, the fingers downward and the back of the hand up. This gesture is often accompanied on the part of the insulter with the typical phrase: *Na! (H)arpa!* ('There! Take it!') This gesture, in Variation No. I, presumably expresses the simple showing of the penis in the direction of the insulted person. Modern Greeks are quite conscious of this symbolism. (See Figure 1.)

**Variation No. II:** When the insulter is not satisfied merely by Variation No. I (Figure 1), he attempts to test and upset the insulted person's calm by means of Variation No. II. In this, both hands move simultaneously and in one violent motion. Before engaging in this violent movement, the insulter spits into the palm of his left hand; then, with angry emotion, he beats on the open and moistened palm of his left hand, with the wrist of the right hand which has already assumed the form of phallic fist. (See Figure 2.) The insulter displays this interlacement of the two hands to the insulted, simultaneously moving the phallic fist up and down several times. This violent gesture is usually accompanied by the standard expression: *Arpa, pousti!* ('Grab that, fag!'), to which the insulted replies or counters at once, with the equally standard phrase: *Ston kōlo sou, malaka!* ('Up your own ass, you jackoff/cunt!') Essentially, Variation No. II depicts an act of rectal coition

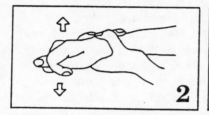

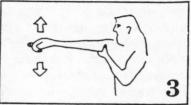

which the insulted must support in imagination, or one that it is presumed he has the ambition to support in reality. The left hand of the insulter represents the anus (moistened, as aforesaid), and the right hand represents the penis.

**Variation No. III:** This is the final and most furious form of the fist-phallus gesture. The insulter's right hand being already in the shape of the fist-phallus, he stretches this arm in the direction of the insulted, meanwhile clapping his left palm up into his right armpit. (See Figure 3.) Variation No. III is tantamount to the insulter threatening the insulted: *Tha ston khōsō etsi olon ton poutso!* ('Thus I will shove my whole prick into you!')

The gesture of the fist-phallus is well known among many peoples outside of Greece. Russians often use Variation No. I, and the French are fond of a gesture similar to Variation No. II. Italians use a form of Variation No. III, in which the left palm strikes not in the right armpit, but on the right biceps, several times, while the right hand's vertical fist-phallus moves up and down, and gyrates with a reaming motion as it rises and falls. This is a whole pacedicatory scenario. The finger displayed as penis in this gesture in Latin countries is not always the thumb, but may be the centre finger: the ancient Roman *digitus impudicus* gesture, now known as 'the finger' in English. Latin peoples also do not always identify the out-thrust thumb in this gesture as the penis. Some pretend it represents the insulted's nose, which has been plucked off by the two fingers and is being 'shown to him'. More seriously it is considered to represent the clitoris, and is therefore a deathly insult when directed at a woman. According to Rabelais it represents a fig in a donkey's anus, which the insulted is being invited to seize with his teeth! This gesture appears as the opening action of Shakespeare's *Romeo and Juliet*, in 1596, where the Montagu and Capulet Italian servants insult each other in this way, under the name of 'biting the thumb': the thumbnail of the Italianate fist-phallus being snapped contemptuously at the insulted under the upper front teeth. A derivative of this gesture is still very much alive in Germanic and English-speaking cultures under the name of 'nose-thumbing', or in German 'the long nose', In its most recent form, whether with one hand, or both – in the latter case the baby-finger of the first hand, and thumb of the second are linked – the element of the out-thrust thumb or finger is modified, and all the fingers are spread wide and even waggled to 'increase' the insult. The gesture in this form approaches another modern Greek gesture of insult or admonition: the *moudza* (μουντζα) or spread-open upraised hand – the older *Vade retro Satanas!* and modern STOP! handsign.

As understood by modern Greek people, the fist-phallus is an indirect or symbolized exposure of the insulter's penis, an exposure intended to humiliate or terrify the insulted. Modern Greeks also have another gesture in which they point almost directly at their genitals. This is known to polite Athenians simply as the vertical gesture, and apparently has no other name. The vertical gesture is very simple: A says something to B, and B wishes to express his disdain of what has been said, or his contempt for A. To do so, B holds the palm of his hand stretched out vertically before him, and brings it down sud-

denly, from the level of his face to that of his genitals. (See Figure 5.) At the same time he shouts: *St'arkhidhia mou!* ('To my balls!') Very rarely, a woman 'of loose morals' will perform this vertical gesture, with the appropriate and fatal phrase expressed as: *Sto mouni mou!* ('To my cunt!')

Finally, I would mention in

passing another form of gestural insult used in Greece. When two underworld characters are conversing intensely, sometimes one of them, with a glance downward at his genitals, will say: *Akous, Apostoli?* ('Are you listening to me, Apostolis?') This is a comic personification of the insulter's penis, who or which is being asked if it has heard what the insulter has said. (Implying again that the insulted is being threatened with paedication.) It should be observed that the name *Apostolis*, here given to the penis, is considered humorous in Greek. This little ceremony or byplay, of the question addressed to the speaker's own penis (which remains prudently silent) is considered, in Greece, to be particularly insulting.

---

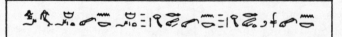

'May you get fucked by a donkey! May your wife get fucked by a donkey! May your child fuck your wife!'

*Legal Curse, Egypt, circa 950* BC

# A GLOSSARY OF ETHNIC SLURS

(Sterling Eisiminger)

To aid the user of this glossary, each main entry begins with the word which identifies the national or ethnic group being maligned. Whenever a comma appears in a main entry, the second element should be read first. Terms like *Zulu princess* and *Tijuana racetrack* have been cross-referenced. Thus *Zulu princess*, for example, is found in its proper alphabetical position among the Z's, but the full entry is found after *blacksmith's shop* since *Zulu* maligns blacks.

**African Railroad:** see listing after **blacksmith's shop**
**Apache:** see listing after **Indian**
**Athenian:** see listing after **Greek side**
**black bagging:** *n.* Pudendum of black women; used collectively
**Black Belt; Black Bottom; Black Town:** *n.* Black community within an urban area
**black bezer:** *n.* Face of a black person
**black jack:** *n.* Black man's penis; homosexual slang
**black joke:** *n.* Pudendum of a black woman
**blackleg:** *n.* Penis of a black man
**black man choke, enough to make a:** *adj. phr.* Very unpalatable; said of food and medicines
**black Maria:** *n.* 1: Black prostitute 2: Pudendum of a black woman
**black meat:** *n.* Pudendum of a black woman
**black mouth:** *n.* Pudendum of a black woman
**black pencil:** *n.* Black man's penis
**blacksmith's shop:** *n.* House of prostitution run by a black woman

112

**African Railroad:** *n.* San Francisco municipal bus line which is principally used by blacks

**Coloured Quarters; Coloured Section; Coloured Settlement; Coloured Town; Coloured Valley:** *n.* Black community within an urban area

**Coon Bottom; Coon Town:** *n.* Black community within an urban area

**Ebony chick; Ebony pidgeon; Ethy meat:** *n.* Black woman; *Ethy* is a clipped form of *Ethiopian*

**Hottentots:** *n.* Buttocks; from the nakedness of these African natives

**Jemima:** *n.* Black woman's pudendum

**Jig Town:** *n.* Black community within an urban area

**jungle meat:** *n.* Black man's penis; homosexual slang

**Nigerian:** *n.* Black man; homosexual slang

**Nigger Hill; Nigger Quarters; Nigger Section; Nigger Town:** *n.* Black community within an urban area

**Nubian:** *n.* Black man; homosexual slang

**pumpernickel:** *n.* [ca. 1924] Black prostitute, especially a mulatto

**Zulu bingo:** *n.* Weekend dancing; homosexual slang

**Zulu princess:** *n.* Young, handsome black man; homosexual slang

**britannia metal:** see listing after **English sentry**

**Canadian; Canadian bacon:** *n.* uncircumcised penis; homosexual slang

**Chinese evil:** *n.* Leprosy; from the prevalence of the disease in China

**Coloured:** see listing after **blacksmith's shop**

**Comanche:** see listing after **Indian**

**Coon:** see listing after **blacksmith's shop**

**Copenhagen:** see listing after **Denmark**

**Corsican:** *n.* Small but effective penis; allusion to Napoleon

**Cuban pumps; Cubans:** *n.* Heavy boots; homosexual slang

**Dago:** see listing after **Italian letter**

**Danish pastry:** *n.* Transsexual; homosexual slang; from the pioneering operation undergone by Christine Jorgensen

**Denmark, something's rotten in:** *cl.* Said of a sex change; homosexual slang

    **Copenhagen capon:** *n.* transsexual; homosexual slang; from the pioneering operation undergone by Christine Jorgensen

    **Copenhagen, go; go to Denmark:** *v. phr.* Have sex-change operation; homosexual slang

**Dutch:** *n.* Wife

**Dutch courage, dry:** *n.* Narcotics; contemporary play on *Dutch courage*

**Dutch dumplings:** *n.* Buttocks; homosexual slang

**Dutch fumigation:** *n.* Resuscitation method learned from American Indians whereby smoke, blown into an animal's bladder, was forced into a victim's rectum to revive him; introduced in England in 1767

**Dutch girl:** *n.* Lesbian; homosexual pun relating *dike* to the dikes of Holland

**Dutch, go:** *v. phr.* Commit suicide

**ebony chick:** see listing after **blacksmith's shop**

**ebony pidgeon:** see listing after **blacksmith's shop**

**Egyptian queen:** *n.* [late 1960s in San Francisco] Homosexual black man, particularly if he is stately and proud

**English martini:** *n.* [late 1960s in San Francisco] Tea, especially when spiked with gin

**English method:** *n.* Homosexual intercourse against the thighs

**English muffins:** *n.* Boy's buttocks; homosexual slang

**English sentry:** *n.* Erect penis

    **britannia metal:** *n.* Sham

**Ethy meat:** *n.* see listing after **blacksmith's shop**

**European accentuation:** *n.* Tapered body with jutting buttocks; homosexual slang

**French:** *v.* To perform fellatio

**French, speak:** *v. phr.* [ca. 1914] Indulge in unconventional sexual play

**French aches:** *n.* [ca. 1700] Syphilis

**French article:** *n.* French prostitute

**French art; French head job; French love:** *n.* Fellatio; homosexual slang

**French bathe:** *v. phr.* To use perfumes as a deodorant in lieu of bathing; homosexual slang

**French by injection:** *adj.* Said of a first-class fellator

**French dip:** *n.* Vaginal precoital fluid; homosexual slang

**French dressing; French-fried ice cream:** *n.* Semen; homosexual slang

**French embassy:** *n.* YMCA with homosexuality running unchecked; homosexual slang

**Frencher:** *n.* Male with a perverse sexual appetite

**Frenchery:** *n.* House of prostitution

**French fare:** *n.* Pudendum of a French woman

**Frenchified:** *adj.* Sexually talented; said of a woman

**Frenchie; French lady; French language expert; French woman:** *n.* Fellator; homosexual

**French joke, tell a:** *v. phr.* Oral stimulation of anus; homosexual slang

**French kiss filter:** *n.* Any filter-tipped cigarette; homosexual slang

**French language training:** *n.* Teaching fellatio; homosexual slang

**French lessons, take:** *v. phr.* Contract venereal disease

**French marbles:** *n.* [ca. 1700] Syphilis

**French measles:** *n.* [ca. 1600] Syphilis

**French mole:** *n.* [ca. 1700] Syphilis

**French photographer:** *n.* Homosexual photographer; homosexual slang

**French postcard:** *n.* Exciting prospective sexual partner; homosexual slang

**French prints:** *n.* Unusual heterosexual pornography; homosexual slang

**French revolution:** *n.* Revolution for homosexual rights; homosexual slang

**French screwdriver:** *n.* Hammer

**French stuff:** *n.* **1:** pornography **2:** unusual sex activity

    **Gallic disease:** *n.* Syphilis

    **Paris brothers:** *n.* Homosexuals, esp. twins; homosexual slang

**Galilee stompers:** *n.* Sandals; homosexual slang

**Gallic disease:** see after **French stuff**

**German helmet:** *n.* Glans penis; homosexual slang
**German marching pills:** *n.* Amphetamines esp. methedrine; homosexual slang
**German silver:** *n.* Sham
**Greek:** *v.* Engage in pederasty; homosexual slang
**Greek, low:** *n.* Sexual intercourse
**Greek love; Greek way:** *n.* Pederasty; homosexual slang
**Greek side:** *n.* Posterior; homosexual slang
  **Athenian:** *n.* Pederast; homosexual slang
  **Trojan horse:** *n.* Manly façade; homosexual slang
**Hawaiian disease:** *n.* Absence of women, or *lakanuki*; homosexual slang
**Hawaiian eye:** *n.* Anus; homosexual slang
  **pineapple princess; pineapple queen:** *n.* Hawaiian homosexual
**Hindustani jig:** *n.* Anal intercourse
**Hottentots:** see listing after **blacksmith's shop**
**Indian, dead as a wooden:** *adj. phr.* Dead
  **Apache:** *n.* Man who uses cosmetics; homosexual slang
  **Comanche:** *n.* Man who uses cosmetics; homosexual slang
  **Indian rug:** *n.* Cheap wig done in braids; homosexual slang
  **Indians, give it back to the:** *v. phr.* said if anything fails or breaks
  **Injun:** *n.* Junior intern
**Irish:** *n.* Sexual temperament or fury
**Irish beauty:** *n.* Woman with black eyes
**Irish clubhouse:** *n.* Refined house of prostitution
**Irish confetti:** *n.* Semen spilled extravaginally
**Irish dip:** *n.* **1:** 'Cure for bashfulness with the girls' **2:** Sexual intercourse
**Irish draperies:** *n.* Pendulous breasts
**Irish fairy:** *n.* Homosexual from the old sod[omy]; homosexual slang
**Irish horse:** *n.* Impotent penis
**Irish legs:** *n.* Heavy female legs
**Irishman, potato-fingered:** *n.* Clumsy person; from the alleged

predilection of the Irish for potatoes and the stereotype of their awkwardness

**Irish marathon:** *n.* Extended session of lovemaking

**Irish pasture:** *n.* Pudendum of an Irish woman

**Irish promotion:** *n.* Masturbation

**Irish rise:** *n.* Sexual detumescence

**Irish toothpick:** *n.* Erect penis of a sodomite

**Irish wedding:** *n.* Masturbation

**Italian airlines:** *n.* Walking; homosexual slang

**Italian fig:** *n.* Poisoned fig used as a secret way to destroy an obnoxious person

**Italian letter:** *n.* [ca. 1870] Condom

> **Dago Center; Dago Town:** *n.* Italian or Puerto Rican community in an urban area
>
> **Neapolitan disease:** Syphilis
>
> **Spaghetti Corner:** *n.* Italian community within an urban area
>
> **Wop Flat; Wop Town:** *n.* Italian community within an urban area

**Jamaica discipline:** *n.* Wife's denial of sexual favors to her husband

**Jemima:** *n.*: see listing after **blacksmith's shop**

**Jew sheet:** *n.* Account, often imaginary, of money lent to friends

**Jew's lance:** *n.* Jewish circumcised penis

**Jew Town:** *n.* Jewish community within an urban area

**Jewish airlines:** *n.* Walking; homosexual slang

**Jewish by hospitalization; Jewish by operation not by nation:** *adj. phr.* Circumcised but not Jewish; homosexual slang

**Jewish compliment; Jewish National:** *n.* Circumcised penis; homosexual slang

**Jewish corned beef:** *n.* Circumcised penis of a Jew

**Jewish dilemma:** *n.* Free ham

**Jewish foreplay:** *n.* Extended pleading without any physical contact

**Jewish lightning:** *n.* Fire insurance; an insurance term for a payment made to someone suspected of torching his own establishment

**Jewish Renaissance:** *n.* Over-elaborate furniture of doubtful
    taste; homosexual slang
        **kipper, young:** *n.* Inadequate meal; play on *Yom Kippur*
        **kosher; kosher style:** *adj.* Circumcised; homosexual slang
        **kosher delicatessen:** *n.* Israel; homosexual slang
        **kosher dill:** *n.* Circumcised penis; homosexual slang
**jig:** see listing after **blacksmith's shop**
**jungle meat:** see listing after **blacksmith's shop**
**kipper, young:** see listing after **Jewish Renaissance**
**kosher:** see listing after **Jewish Renaissance**
**Latin mystery:** *n.* Doctor's prescription
**Mexican airlines, to fly:** *v. phr.* Smoke marijuana; from the
    fact that much marijuana smoked in the US is grown in
    Mexico
**Mexican cigarette:** *n.* Poorly made marijuana cigarette; homo-
    sexual slang
**Mexican hairless:** *n.* Bald head
**Mexican jumping bean:** *n.* Amphetamine; homosexual slang
**Mexican nightmare:** *n.* Gaudy ceramic crockery; homosexual
    slang
**Mexican schlock:** *n.* Any art in poor taste; homosexual slang
        **tamale** *n.* Gaudy ceramic crockery; homosexual slang
        **Tijuana Bible:** *n.* Lurid pornography
        **Tijuana racetrack:** *n.* Diarrhoea run; homosexual slang
**Neapolitan disease:** see listing after **Italian letter**
**Nigerian:** see listing after **blacksmith's shop**
**nigger:** see listing after **blacksmith's shop**
**Nubian:** see listing after **blacksmith's shop**
**Paris brothers:** see listing after **French stuff**
**pineapple:** see listing after **Hawaiian eye**
**Polack:** see listing after **Polish handball**
**Polish airlines:** *n.* Walking; homosexual slang
**Polish disease:** *n.* [ca. 1700] Syphilis
**Polish handball:** *n.* Dried nasal mucus; homosexual slang
        **Polack Town:** *n.* Polish community within an urban area
**pumpernickel:** see listing after **blacksmith's shop**
**Quaker guns:** *n.* Logs painted to look like guns during US Civil
    War; so named because of Quaker pacifism

**redneck:** see listing after **white-meat**

**Roman candle:** *n.* **1:** Italian-American penis **2:** Any Italian; homosexual slang

**Roman engagement:** *n.* Anal intercourse with a virgin girl; homosexual slang

**Roman historian:** *n.* Orgy enthusiast; homosexual slang

**Roman night:** *n.* Orgy; homosexual slang

**Rome, fountains of:** *n.* Urinals; homosexual slang

**Russian, high:** *n.* Simultaneous fellatio and anal intercourse; homosexual slang

**Russian salad party:** *n.* Orgy in which all participants are greasy; homosexual slang

**Russian, white:** *n.* Oral exchange of semen; homosexual slang

**Scotch screw:** *n.* Nocturnal emission

**Spaghetti:** see listing after **Italian letter**

**Spanish cure:** *n.* Treatment of drug addiction by forced total abstinence

**Spanish fig:** *n.* Poisoned fig used as a secret way to destroy an obnoxious person

**Spanish rice:** *n.* Lumpy semen; homosexual slang

**Sweden, product of:** *n.* Artificial blond homosexual; homosexual slang

**tamale:** see listing after **Mexican schlock**

**Tijuana:** see listing after **Mexican schlock**

**Trojan:** see listing after **Greek side**

**Turkish delight:** *n.* Pederasty; homosexual slang

**Turkish disease:** *n.* [ca. 1500] Syphilis

**Viking queen:** *n.* **1:** blond **2:** Blond male homosexual; homosexual slang

**white-man's disease:** *n.* Relative inability of Caucasians to jump; blacks' term of derision usually used in a basket-ball context

**white meat; white owl:** *n.* White man's penis; homosexual slang

> **redneck foreplay:** *n.* Complete absence of any preliminary physical contact
>
> **Yankee:** *n.* Masturbation; homosexual slang; from *yank off* meaning 'to masturbate'

**Yankee's yawn:** *n.* Open mouth of climaxing male; homosexual slang

**Wop:** see listing after **Italian letter**

**Yankee:** see listing after **white-meat**

**Zulu:** see listing after **blacksmith's shop**

---

STATE OF CALIFORNIA
PROPOSITION 63

That English – you know, *English*, the language? OK. That it, I mean English (the language) would be, like the totally *official* language. I mean, in California. And everybody would have to, like speak it and everything. In California.

☐ Fer shure!            ☐ No way, José!

---

How do you pick out the Irish dykes at a lesbian convention?
– *They're the ones picking up men.*

Why didn't the little Greek boy run away from home?
– *Because he couldn't leave his brothers behind.*

What's a Jewish porno film?
– *Ten minutes of sex and 50 minutes of guilt.*

# TALK DIRTY TO ME AGAIN:
## MORE SEXY SLOGANS

(Reinhold Aman)

Be kind to animals. Take a bitch to dinner
Born-again bitch
Feel safe tonight. Sleep with a cop
Having sex is like playing bridge. If you don't have a good
   partner, you'd better have a good hand
I don't have an eating problem. I eat. I get fat. I buy new
   clothes. No problem
If I wanted to hear from an asshole I would have farted!
Instant asshole . . . just add alcohol
It would be easy for me to make it hard for you
Life is a bed of roses, but watch out for the pricks
Life is like a shit sandwich. The more bread you have, the less
   shit you have to eat
Life's a bitch and then you die
Life's a bitch, then you marry one
Moody bitch seeks a kind, considerate guy for a love-hate
   relationship
The person wearing this shirt is a police officer. Lie flat on your
   back and do everything the nice officer tells you
Wanted: Meaningful overnight relationship
What are you staring at, dickhead?
Women like the simplest things in life . . . men
Yes . . . but not with you
You don't know anything about a woman until you meet her
   in court!
You're twisted, perverted & sick. I like that in a person
Your father should have pulled out early

# IS FRENCH A SEXIST LANGUAGE?
# DOING CUNTERIES IN FRANCE

(Andrew R Sisson)

France beckons to us eternally. Alpine skiing at Chamonix or Val d'Isère. A Norman castle or a Loire château. The azure Riviera. And Paris calls us at any time of the year.

Ah, *la belle France*, cultural mother of us all! Seat of rational thought, of refined eating, drinking and fashion in the modern world. Even etiquette itself – good manners as a ticket of entry to sophistication and wealth – is a French invention, although surely the Orientals have their own view of the matter. But beware, you not-so-cunning linguists, of the French tongue as she is really spoken. You are in for a major culture shock. Take out your pocket dictionary – but first of all – listen! In France nowadays, it is fashionable to call everybody a 'cunt'. Yes, a cunt, or *con*, meaning a stupid or dumb person of either sex. Anti-feminist? Not at all. *Il est con; elle est con; ça, c'est vraiment con* have no sexual cunnotation. They simply mean 'dumb' or 'stupid'. And liberated French girls use this all-purpose noun/adjective just as frequently as their brothers. (The dictionary adjectives for 'dumb' are *bête* and *stupide*, but they are seldom used.)

*Con* is not an insult in our English sense. For *us* to call someone a 'cunt' or a 'dumb cunt' constitutes a crude sexist remark. One envisages a void, ambulatory vagina. After all, are men 'cunts' or women 'pricks'? We smile at the absurdity. No way. And English has a variety of put-down vocabulary to delve into. Examples:

A. Profanity: *goddamn, Jesus Christ*
B. Dubious ancestry references: *son of a bitch, bastard*

122

C. Barnyard words: *ass, shit, piss, fuck*
D. Recent Yiddish enrichments: *schlemiel, schnook, schmuck.*

Most recently we have been using *cunt* in a sexy way, in the tell-it-like-it-is prose of today. A sexy genital reference, as in 'her hairy, bushy, warm, wet, soft *cunt*'. Not a *person* cunt, but an *organ* cunt. Much nicer than a collective 'bunch of cunt' or the 'wet split beaver' of Garp's fantasies in John Irving's novel.

How then can the French be so crude, so gross? *Il est con, elle est con, c'est un vrai con.* How can these supposed masters or mistresses of all things refined and cultivated talk that way? Didn't they practically invent sex as a recreational sport in Europe? Aren't 'French kissing' and 'Frenching' their discoveries? No, but we like to give them credit – or blame – just as national or ethnic chauvinism leads the English to call the male prophylactic a 'French letter' and their Gallic cousins to dub same rubber sheath *capot anglaise*, 'English raincoat'. As in the following ditty, spoken by *madame* or *mademoiselle*:

> Chéri, quand tu me baises
> Ne porte pas la capote anglaise:
> Quand tu termines, c'est tellement doux
> De sentir couler les bons jus.

> Darling, when you fuck me
> Don't wear a rubber:
> When you finish it's so sweet
> To feel the good juices flow.

Needless to say, the lady is not talking about roast beef with gravy, *au jus.*

We know that 'cunt' and *con* derive from the Latin *cunnus* (vulva) and *cuneus* (wedge), as in 'cuneiform' or wedge-shaped writing. But most of the younger French who call each other *con* are apparently unaware of this fact, or of the fact that *con* refers literally to female genitalia. In any case, listen for the ubiquitous little syllable (sounds like 'cawn', more or less) on your next trip to Gaul. French youth has a far richer slang than we – or the Germans – for everyday activities, such as eating, drinking, working or sleeping. Teenagers can talk for hours in a tongue almost incomprehensible to their elders, to say nothing of foreign visitors. Frequently heard expressions include *vachement*, *mec*, and *chiant*, best translated as 'terribly', 'guy/dude', and 'shitty'. French is far too heavily salted and peppered, nevertheless, by that overused wordlet *con*. It is perhaps even more prevalent than the World War II American all-purpose adjective *fucking*, and its British equivalent, *bloody*. (*Bloody* comes from 'by Our Lady' and is thus profane in origin, but its users remain, for the most part, blissfully ignorant of such sources.) The French have another word for vulva as 'pussy': it is *chatte*, or female cat, proving that visions of vulvas as feline and furry leap over language barriers. As for the French origin of *bastard*, they use this noun (*bâtard*) very seldom and in its literal sense of illegitimacy, or as a synonym for *petit pain* or small loaf of bread.

Variations on the theme of *con* abound, and you will hear them in ski lines, in village cafés, on beaches, and especially where the language of youth is spoken – in films, on TV, in magazines and novels. *Elle fait des conneries. Il fait des conneries.* How marvellous! 'To make cunteries', meaning 'to do stupid things'. In true Gallic logic, *le con*, 'cunt', is masculine and *la bitte*, 'prick', is feminine; but no matter. There's no logic in language.

---

Why do Jewish women use golden diaphragms?
– *Because they want their men to come into money.*

Name a biceptual athlete.
– *Arnold Schwarzenegger.*

# OFFENSIVE LANGUAGE VIA COMPUTER

(Reinhold Aman)

Computer networks can be used to gather information from throughout the world. Unlike in traditional fieldwork, one does not have to interview informants personally but simply posts a query, or an entire questionnaire, on the electronic bulletin board (BB), and the users respond. BB's make this novel way of collecting data and responding easy: one calls the BB's number and leaves one's response. The quality and range of the responses depend on the precision of the questions asked, as well as on the type of user. Naturally, one can ask only those who have a computer and modem, which severely restricts the field of informants. However, these informants can gather information locally from those lacking such equipment and send it to the BB.

Henry Birdseye's 'The Unknown BBS' is such a system for collecting information. It runs at 300 and 1200 baud and contains about one-quarter million characters' worth of kakological riddles, jokes, and other offensive language.

To test the usefulness of his system, Mr Birdseye asked his BB users about terms for masturbation, urination, and vomiting. He did not request other essential information from the informants, such as their sex, age, geographic location, education, profession, etc, but the simple data below prove that such a BB system can be used successfully. To transmit the information gathered to others, one can either call up the BB and download it (have it sent by telephone to one's own computer), or ask for a printout, which I did. Following below are the terms, after organizing and alphabetizing the raw data.

125

**to masturbate** (of females): beat the beaver, buttonhole, clap your clit, cook cucumbers, grease the gash, hide the hotdog, hit the slit, hose your hole, juice your sluice, make waves [from 'the (little) man in the boat' = clitoris?], pet the poodle, slam the clam, stump-jump.

**to masturbate** (of males): beat the bishop, beat your little brother, beat the meat, burp the worm, butter your corn, choke the chicken, clean your rifle, consult Dr Jerkoff, crank your shank, dink your slinky, feel in your pocket for your big hairy rocket, file your fun-rod, fist your mister, flex your sex, flog the dolphin, flog your dog, grease your pipe, hack your mack, hump your hose, jerkin' the gherkin, milk the chicken, Onan's Olympics (*n.*), one-stick drum improvisation (*n.*), pack your palm, paint your ceiling, play a flute solo on your meat whistle, play the male organ, please your pisser, point your social finger, polish your sword, pound the pud, pound your flounder, prompt your porpoise, prune the fifth limb, pull the pope, pull your taffy, run your hand up the flagpole, shine your pole, shoot the tadpoles, slakin' the bacon, slam your hammer, slam your Spam, slap your wapper, spank the monkey, spank the salami, strike the pink match, stroke the dog, stroke your poker, talk with Rosy Palm and her five little sisters, tickle your pickle, thump your pumper, tweak your twinkie, unclog the pipes, varnish your pole, walk the dog, watch the eyelid movies, wax your dolphin, whip your dripper, whizzin' jizzum, wonk your conker, yang your wang, yank the yam, yank your crank.

**to urinate**: bleed the liver, drain the dragon, drain the (main) vein, get rid of the bladder matter, siphon the python, visit Miss Murphy.

**to vomit**: drive the big white bus, hug the porcelain, kneel before the porcelain throne, pray to the porcelain gods, school lunch rerun (*n.*), technicolour rerun (*n.*), upchuck.

# CLEVER DOGS

A painter, an electrician, a plumber and a train driver were sitting in a café, discussing how smart their dogs were. The painter said his dog could do maths. He told his dog, named T-Square, to go to the blackboard and draw a square, a circle and a triangle; which the dog did with no sweat.

The electrician said he thought his dog Slide Rule was better. Slide Rule was told to fetch a dozen chocolate biscuits and divide them into 4 piles of 3; which Slide Rule did with no problems.

The plumber said that was good, but his dog was even better. His dog Measure was told to get a pint of milk and pour 3 oz into a 7 oz glass. The dog did this without any difficulty. All three men agreed this was very good and that all the dogs were smart.

Then they turned to the train driver and said, 'What can *your* dog do?' The train driver called his dog and said, 'Show the lads what you can do, Coffee Break.' Coffee Break went over and pissed on the blackboard, ate the chocolate biscuits, drank the milk, fucked the other three dogs, claimed he injured his back doing it, filed for compensation and left for home on sick leave.

# TORSO JOKES

What do you call a man with no arms and no legs . . . who's helping to change a tyre?
– *Jack*.

. . . who gets left behind in a restaurant?
– *Tip*.

. . . who comes in your letter-box?
– *Bill*.

. . . who's been dropped into the ocean?
– *Bob*.

. . . in a nudist colony?
– *Seymore*.

. . . flying over the fence?
– *Homer*.

. . . painted with sunsets?
– *Van*.

. . . who's been thrown across the surface of a pond?
– *Skip*.

. . . who's been nailed to the wall?
– *Art*.

. . . with a bad cold?
– *Fleming*.

. . . who's been run over by a steamroller?
– *Miles*.

# COMMON PATIENT-DIRECTED PEJORATIVES USED BY MEDICAL PERSONNEL

(C J Scheiner)

All professions have a slang which serves to convey a large amount of information or an entire situation in a shorthand form. Negative feelings or situations can be expressed verbally, and often very colourfully, through the use of pejoratives which, if they are incorporated into a professional slang, become part of a semi-secret vocabulary that reinforces a sense of solidarity and separation from others not of the particular profession.

Two conditions anger physicians and medical personnel in particular: (1) patients who do not follow medical advice, and (2) patients who do not respond as expected to medical therapy. The former may be considered a defiance of authority, while the latter is a reminder of the limitations of the medical practitioner.

The following is a short list of commonly encountered pejoratives directed against patients, collected from oral use in a large hospital in New York, from 1976 to 1978. The list does not include terms as commonly used by non-medical personnel, for example *stupid* or *creep*, nor does it include pejoratives that simply incorporate medically related terms. eg *spineless* or *shithead*. This study is not in any way exhaustive, and does not include many terms used possibly in various specialty areas of this particular hospital, and certainly not all the terms used in various hospitals in or outside of New York.

**Botanist:** see **Veterinarian**
**Crock:** a patient who medically abuses himself, often with

alcohol. Either short for 'crock of shit' or from 'crocked' = drunk

**Dispo**: a patient admitted to the hospital with no real medical problem other than being unable to care for himself/herself in his/her present circumstances. Short for 'disposition problem'

**Ethanolic**: an alcoholic

**FOS**: abbreviation for 'full of shit'. **1**: a severely constipated patient, often impacted with months of unpassed faeces **2**: a patient who lies to gain medically unnecessary drugs

**Fruit Salad**: a group of stroke patients, all totally unable to care for themselves. See **Vegetable**

**Geologist**: see **Veterinarian**

**Gork**: a mentally deficient patient, either congenitally, secondary to chronic drug or alcohol abuse, or following a cerebral contusion or bleed. Also, 'to heavily sedate'

**Gorked Out**: semi-comatose

**Gun and Rifle Club**: a trauma ward to which stabbing and gunshot victims are admitted

**Hotdog**: a flamboyant or bizarre patient, usually with psychiatric problems

**HYS**: abbreviation for 'hysterical'

**International House of Pancakes**: a neurology ward occupied by patients, often stroke victims, all of whom babble in different languages

**Loxed**: a decreased state of consciousness, usually following a cardiac or respiratory arrest. Contraction for 'lack of oxygen'. Also, 'loxed out'

**No Squash**: a condition of irreparable brain damage, most often from trauma, intracranial haemorrhage, drug abuse, or prolonged anoxia; see **Vegetable Garden**

**OD**: abbreviation for 'overdose'. A particularly despised patient, as the cause of this malady is self-induced

**Pits**: the medical screening area of a hospital, particularly hated by physicians because of the enormous amounts of insignificant medical maladies that must be treated there in a hospital setting. Also known as the **Screaming Area**

**PMD**: abbreviation for 'private medical doctor'. A physician who refers his apparently ill patients to the hospital Emergency Room rather than diagnose and treat them himself. This is one of the few pejoratives directed at a member of the professional group

**POS:** abbreviation for 'piece of shit'. A general term for patients medically ill because of their own failure to care for themselves (most often alcoholics)

**Potato Patch:** see **Vegetable Garden**

**PP:** abbreviation for 'professional patient'. A person who appears regularly, either daily or weekly, at the Emergency Room for trivial complaints such as the refill of innocuous medicines or the treatment of chronic symptoms that are never present at the time of examination

**PPP:** abbreviation for 'piss-poor protoplasm'. A debilitated patient, often requiring surgery, who needs extensive medical treatment, including transfusions, before he is able to undergo definitive therapy

**Quack:** a patient who fakes symptoms to gain unnecessary hospitalization or drugs

**Rose Garden:** see **Vegetable Garden**

**Saturday Night Special:** a patient, usually an alcoholic, who has spent his money, and comes to the hospital at the weekend looking for a meal and a place to stay

**Schizo:** short for 'schizophrenic'. Any mentally abnormal patient

**Screamer:** a hysterical patient

**Screaming Area:** see **Pits**

**Scut:** menial medical procedures that must be carried out, usually relegated to the least senior member of the medical team. Also, any patient held in extremely low esteem

**SHPOS:** acronym for 'sub-human piece of shit.' A chronic POS. A critically ill patient who, after intensive medical care and rehabilitation, fails to follow medical instructions, and is readmitted to the hospital in his previous critical condition

**Stage Mother:** an adult who coaches younger patients as to their alleged symptoms, and generally states what medical tests and procedures are necessary

**Stroked Out:** in a state of decreased consciousness and muscular ability following a cerebral bleed

**Subway Rider:** a patient who comes to the Emergency Room with minor or non-existing medical complaints as a means to getting free subway fare home

**Turkey:** a patient with a trivial medical complaint

**Two-Carbon Abuser:** An alcoholic. From the chemical formula for alcohol, $C_2 H_6 O$ ($C_2 = 2$ carbon atoms)

**Vegetable:** a neurologically depressed patient, usually as result of a stroke, who is totally unable to care for himself. Also called **potato, carrot, cucumber,** or the name of any other specific vegetable or plant

**Vegetable Garden:** a group of unconscious or semi-conscious patients. Also known as **Rose Garden, Potato Patch,** etc

**Veterinarian:** a physician who considers his patients of less than human intelligence. Related terms: **Botanist:** an MD with patients of less than animal intelligence; and **Geologist:** an MD with patients of absolutely no intelligence

**Water the Garden:** to change the intravenous bottles that serve as the sole source of nourishment for severely neurologically impaired patients

---

*Editor's Note:* As reported in the *Süddeutsche Zeitung* (Germany) of 19 April 1978, page 13, verbal abuse of the patients by physicians also exists in Germany. Professor Dr Albert Göb, head of the spastics centre in Munich, is involved in a major scandal caused in part by his continuous verbal attacks on the 300 handicapped youths at the centre. He calls them *Deppen* (dopes), *Idioten* (idiots), *blöde Deppen* (stupid idiots), *Kartoffelköpfe* (potatoheads), and *Dummköpfe* (dumbheads).

# SOME EXAMPLES OF THE HISTORICAL INSULT GRIEVOUS IN CONTEMPORARY IRELAND

(Fiach Ó Broin)

The Irish memory is incredibly long. We are just beginning to accept as natives those Norman-French families who first came here as invaders in the twelfth century. Personal insults which really sting can often refer back into the misty past.

The informer or turncoat is a universally-despised figure. In Ireland, more often than not, the family of one of these people has had to carry the stigma long after the originator of it has died. In most cases the immediate family has given in and emigrated eventually. To suggest there is 'informer's blood' in a family is literally fighting talk. The classic example is one Patrick Carey, who turned state's evidence on a group of patriotic assassins with whom he was involved in 1882. He was afterwards provided with new identity, passport, and what have you, but was none the less 'executed' in a steamer off Cape Town shortly after his erstwhile companions were hanged. So, if one wants to raise a row with someone surnamed Carey, the mere suggestion that they might be related to this man is enough.

Another example of this type of insult that springs to mind is that of Dermot Mac Murrough, who brought in the Normans. This family slur was so potent that the surname is almost unknown nowadays. What is done is that an alternate anglicised version of it – Murphy – is used instead. In fact it is the single commonest Irish surname. For the record, Mac Murrough died in 1172.

Whole counties are still slighted for the part their inhabitants played in the Rebellion of 1798. Corkmen are disliked on sight in Wexford as the Cork Militia put down the rising in that county. Given Irish memories, what a man's forebear did in 1916 or earlier is fairly common knowledge.

In Skerries, 20 miles north of Dublin, the supreme method of insult is to ask about goats. 'Is there goat on the menu today?' or 'Have you eaten goat recently?' means trouble. Legend has it that St Patrick came to Skerries in AD 440 or thereabouts and left his pet goat on the mainland while he went off to meditate on an islet off the coast. When he got back, the goat had been eaten. In the early 1950s, Cork stone-sculptor Seamus Murphy was commissioned to do a statue of St Pat to stand outside the local church in Skerries. As he was depicting the good Saint with his bishop's crozier in his hand, he wanted something else on his off-side to balance the work. He came across a reference to St Patrick's pet goat and, in all innocence, included it in the finished work. There was a near riot at the unveiling, and Murphy had to re-veil the statue and chip off the goat.

For a Clareman, one suggests he is not speaking too clearly: 'Speak up, and take the wool out from between your teeth' or some such phrase. The reference is to the story (I don't know whether true or false) that the Clare farmers castrated their rams with their teeth.

In various towns and districts, particularly on the East Coast, Skerries again, or Rush, Howth, Wicklow, or Tory Island in the far north, or in some areas of West Cork, a casual reference to 'wreckers' will bring rapid reaction. Smugglers and pirates were always halfway respected if not respectable; but those who put 'false lights' out to wreck ships have always been regarded as the lowest of the low. The above towns and districts were known as bases for this trade.

'The curse of Cromwell on you!' still lives on as a strong malediction. If you want to suggest Ironside descent in an Irishman, pick someone a lot smaller than you, considerably less fit, and preferably hard-of-hearing. The touchiest area for this type of comment is around Drogheda, a town which was sacked and its inhabitants massacred by the Cromwellians in 1649. But this happened at the end of a long hard campaign, and discipline was slipping by then. The Irish had sent most of their womenfolk out of the town before the siege, and the Roundheads 'had their way' with them either by force, or in return for food as often as not. Two years ago I heard a man who lived 15 miles from the place say, 'Work in Drogheda? Not I. Sure, there's nothing in that place but Cromwell's bastards.' A parallel reference will get your head broken in the Aran Islands, too. This is because a Cromwellian garrison was left there, which may have intermarried with the natives.

A small townland in County Mayo – Coillte Mághach – is the back of beyond in Ireland. The English spelling varies but the pronunciation is 'kill-cheh maw-ukh'. In its shortened form, *culchie*, it is derogatory for a 'country bumpkin'. Harmless enough in most cases, but not in front of a Mayoman.

The inland county of Cavan has two interesting dialect expressions. A *hayveril* (spelling?) is someone either 'not all there' or 'still a bit rough around the edges'. It comes from the Irish *aimhearál* ('av-orr-awl') – something raw or uncooked. *Djawskin* is for an 'unlettered rustic', and is local pronunciation of the eighteenth-century slang English *joskin*, a 'rube' (Grose's *Dictionary of the Vulgar Tongue*). Cavan people are famed as pennypinchers, and a saying has it, 'When a Cavan man comes to Dublin, two Jews leave.'

If you really like a whiff of length of memory, the ideal example is Tory Island, off the North Donegal coast. Rumour still has it that the island was never properly or fully Christianized, and that there's more than a touch of pagan savagery about the islanders to this day. An offhand 'Is there a church here?' will bring reactions varying from suspicion to murderous rage, depending on the tone and nuance with which it's delivered.

---

How can you spot an Italian airplane?
– *Look for hair under its wings.*

# DIALOGUE GRAFFITI

(Professor Rudolf Schmid)

The following chain of graffiti, most of them written by different hands, was copied verbatim from the men's room (third floor) in the Life Sciences Building at the University of California, Berkeley, 2 August 1985:

The sultry bitch with the fiery eyes
*The bulky bitch with thunderous thighs*
The horny bitch who goes for guys
*The topless bitch who digs French fries*
The unwashed bitch who attracts flies
*The romantic bitch with the lonesome sighs*
The executive bitch with the striped ties
*The ugly bitch who nevertheless tries*
The not-cooking bitch who makes my bread rise
*The sleezy bitch who the prudes despise*
The robot bitch you computerize
*The oriental bitch with slanted eyes*
The rich bitch who always buys
*The feminist bitch who will circumcise*
The micro bitch who seduces flies
*There's not a hitch to this misogynist kitsch*
The transvestite bitch to the mensroom hies
*The racist bitch for redneck guys*
The post-doc bitch who ain't so wise
*The starry-eyed bitch with the warehouse eyes*
The vampire bitch who never dies
*The gorgon bitch who petrifies*
The prostitute bitch who her trade plies

*The warm-fronted bitch with the overcast skies*
The falsy-topped bitch whose outline's a lie
*The dead bitch who grossly putrifies*
The AIDS tainted bitch was my slow demise
*The Nympho-bitch with the orgasmic cries*

---

How can you tell that a woman is wearing tights?
– *When she farts, her ankles swell up.*

What do you call a gay Jew?
– *A Heblew.*

How do you bathe Haitians?
– *You don't. You just let them wash up on shore.*

What do you call a beautiful girl in Poland?
– *Tourist.*

How did Helen Keller's parents punish her?
– *They rearranged the furniture.*

# AIRBORN(E) BULLSHIT

One stormy night, when visibilities and ceilings were pushing minimums, aircraft flights were being stacked up all over the terminal areas. The inordinate delays and the incessant holding patterns were starting to unnerve both pilots and ground controllers. A few pilots started to hound Air Traffic Control for immediate descent and approach clearances. One intrepid but harassed controller had his fill, and snarled into the microphone on a frequency heard by most of the impatient crews, 'I'll get you guys down as soon as I can. We are doing the best we know how.'

A slight silence, and then an unidentified voice loudly uttered a caustic but effective vulgarism, '**Bullshit!**'

The controller took offence at the language and barked officiously, 'Attention all flights! Who said that!?'

After a dramatic pause, one by one, the pious denials came in with standard but bizarre phraseology:

> '*British Midland 345*: Negative on the bullshit.'
> '*Swissair 52*: Negative on the bullshit.'
> '*Aer Lingus 302*: Negative on the bullshit.'
> '*Continental 602*: Negative on the bullshit.'
> '*Delta 410*: Negative on the bullshit.'
> '*Qantas 002*: Negative on the bullshit.'

# JAPANESE SEXUAL MALEDICTA

(John Solt)

The following sample of Japanese 'bad words' is translated into English for the first time. I selected them for poetic quality and rounded them out with some musts.

Poetry continues to shape the language as it has through the 1200-year history of Japanese literature. On the whole, Japanese in conversation relate rhythmically and with ambiguous gaps – poetic techniques – rather than through prosy recourse to logical exposition. The vast body of Japanese poetry written with hidden allusions to the past is an example of the vivid manner in which the tradition is kept alive, as is the frequent recourse to proverbs even by labourers.

During the years I lived in Japan (1974–1980), I jotted down colourful words and sayings whenever they caught my attention. Most foreigners believe that Japanese is sparse in maledicta, which is not true. However, they can be quite subtle at times and tend to bypass square-heads conditioned to blunt ravings of the 'up yours, shithead, motherfucker' variety.

Japanese maledicta are less direct than those of other countries because subversive language and thought had to be concealed during the time Japan was isolated from the outside world (Edo period, 1600–1868), when the intellectually and financially superior merchants were stratified socially on the bottom rung, below the samurai, farmers, and artisans. Therefore, in order to capture some of the sophistication of the maledicta of old and modern Japan, I have included not only the abusive side of language but also encrypted and symbolic language which alludes to sexuality.

139

豆腐の角に頭をぶつけて死んしまえ

**Tofu no kado ni atama o butsukete shinde shimae!**

'Go knock your head on a corner of *tofu* and die!' Although
spoken in anger, this expression is not very hostile because
*tofu* (bean curd) is softer than marshmallow and would
cause no damage to a bumped head

千擦り

**Senzuri:** 'One thousand rubs': Male masturbation

万擦り

**Manzuri:** 'Ten thousand rubs': Masturbation performed by
females. *The Hite Report*, in which some women attest to
masturbating for up to five hours, confirms that women's
genital self-play is more time-consuming than male masturbation

にわとり

**Niwatori:** 'Chicken': This is a current slang word for a man
who prematurely ejaculates, likened to a chicken ner-
vously flapping its wings

早漏

**Sōrō:** 'Fast leak': A man who ejaculates prematurely

朝うらのにぬ男に金貸すな.

**Asamara no tatanu otoko ni kane kasuna:** 'Never lend money
to a man who doesn't have a hard-on in the morning':
This proverb from the southwestern island of Kyushu has
a practical intention at its base; if he doesn't have an
erection in the morning, he isn't healthy and will probably
die before repaying the money

スケベイ

**Sukebe:** 'Lusty': Every Japanese is familiar with the saying that
the three lustiest groups of 'dirty old men' are doctors,
teachers, and monks. From an Edo fiction character

痴漢

**Chikan:** 'Sexual grabber': As with pinching in Italy, and
exacerbated by crowded trains, illegal grabbing of flesh

abounds in Japan. A few years ago there was a poster campaign around parks and dark alleys warning of *chikan*, depicted with a wolf's head

壷洗い

**Tsubo arai**: 'Jug-washing': Douching. The vagina is seen as an upside-down jug

おまんこに豚の足を突込んで.奥歯がガがガ云わせてやる.

**Omanko ni buta no ashi o tsukkonde okuba gata-gata iwasete yaru!**: 'I'll stick a pig's leg up your cunt until your back-teeth rattle!': This expression is most frequently uttered by cuckolded men and *yakuza* withdrawing from hard drugs. *Yazuka* are the 'Japanese mafia'. They often shoot speed and sometimes are jailed for it. If they violate their own code, they can apologize by having a small finger chopped off.

おまんこ

**Omanko**: 'Cunt': The word *manko* (in dialect, *meko*) is used mostly by men and prostitutes. Other women usually refer to their vulva indirectly as *asoko*, 'there'. As with countless other nouns in Japanese, an *o-* is prefixed to exalt the object in respect, or to denigrate it ironically

ちんこ

**Chinko**: 'Cock': Maybe because of its similarity in sound to the baby-talk word for penis, *chin-chin*, 'pee-pee, wee-wee', *chinko* is less taboo than *manko*. The English word 'penis', mispronounced 'pay-ness', is currently used as frequently as its Japanese counterpart, especially by men

磯巾着

**Isoginchaku**: 'A clam that shrivels': Euphemism for vulva and round coin purses which, when squeezed, open their slit

一杯そば

**Ippai soba:** 'One cup noodle': A noodle-cup fuck. Dehydrated noodles are sold in a styrofoam cup, needing only hot water and a few minutes before they are soft enough to be eaten. Over the last ten years, school boys have developed the practice of cutting out the styrofoam bottom and filling the cup with lukewarm water. As the noodles soften, the penis is inserted and 'goes at it'

随喜の涙を流す.

**Zuiki no namida o nagasu:** 'To let flow tears of zuiki': The Shogun employed various methods to control the populace during the centuries of seclusion: boats large enough to sail to foreign lands were forbidden to be built; people caught trying to enter or exit Japan (except accredited foreigners) were killed; barriers were set up between provinces, and one needed reasons and papers to travel; provincial lords (*daimyō*) were kept hostage in Edo (Tokyo) for long periods of time to ensure their allegiance. When arriving in the capital, the *daimyō* offered the Shogun famous products of their region. The *daimyō* from the province of Higo (present-day Kumamoto) brought *higo-zuiki*, 'cock-rings' and dildos made from the pliant *zuiki* plant, which secretes an itch-causing juice. A mild Spanish fly, the *zuiki* is reputed to have caused the Shogun's numerous concubines to flow orgasmic tears of joy. The expression is innocently used in the sense of 'happy as a lark', because few who utter it are aware of the derivation. In these days of rabbit-headed, three-pronged, battery-operated vibrators and other paraphernalia available in Japanese porn shops (*otona no omochaya*, lit. 'adult toys shop'), the *higo-zuiki* seem relatively tame stimuli

義理まん

**Giri-man:** 'Obligation-cunt': A wife allowing herself to be fucked on an off-night. Women were traditionally expected to take care of their husband's sexual needs even when their own were not aroused. There is no corresponding term of 'obligation-cock'

ス 、八

**Shakuhachi:** 'Bamboo flute': The common word for fellatio. On the other hand, or mouth, the word for cunnilingus is *hamōnika*, 'harmonica', derived from this Western musical instrument that produces pleasant sounds when tongue and lips are moved correctly

エ ッ 千

**Etchi:** 'Pervert': From the pronunciation of the letter *h*, the first letter in romanized script of *hentai*, 'pervert', The idea of using the abbreviated Roman letter of a transcribed Japanese word gives this expression a certain uniqueness, helping its spread

金 玉

**Kintama:** 'Golden balls': Commonly used by men to refer to their testicles. According to the well-known feminist poet in Tokyo, Sachiko Yoshihara, 'No woman would call them golden or silver, just balls'

の ぞ き

**Nozoki:** 'Peeping Tom': The great lovers, from the earliest Japanese novels of one thousand years ago to the present, have all been avid peepers. Partly because of the non-fortification of ancient Japanese architecture and partly because peeping is not considered a sin (as defined by the Christian West), voyeurism has been viewed favourably – or at least tolerated – as only slightly naughty. In fact, in Tokyo in the early eighties the latest sex craze was peeping-tom parlours (*nozokiba*). The peeper enters a closet-size room containing a chair, a box of tissues, and a tiny crevice to gaze through. In the dim light of the main room a lady makes herself up, surrounded by about 20 small closets. A recording informs the customers that she cannot see those peeping on her. The light increases, and she dances around, presses her body against the various slots, and performs *manzuri* ('10,000 rubs') on the carpet, accompanied by the recorded sounds of a female moaning orgasmically

一寸八分の觀音様.

**Issun hachibu no kannon-sama:** 'A *kannon* of 1 *sun* 8 *bu* measurement': Kannon (goddess of mercy) was the Indian Bodhisattva (helper of Buddha) with moustache who was considered male or asexual in China, but was thought of as asexual or female in Japan. This sex change performed on Kannon by Japanese culture through centuries, as well as the native Shinto religious belief that the highest deity, the sun (*amaterasu*), is a woman, have led psychological anthropologists to claim that Japan is a female (mother) oriented society. One *sun*, an archaic measurement, is less than one inch, and 10 *bu* equal one *sun*. In Edo slang, this miniature goddess, about $1\frac{1}{2}$ inches high, represented the clitoris in size, shape, and concept. It specifically refers to the image housed at Asakusa Temple.

The fingers of an open hand (thumb facing up). Each finger represents the angle of a man's erect penis during a decade of his life: during his twenties/thirties, etc.

20 yrs · 30 yrs · 40 yrs · 50 yrs · 60 yrs

The author appreciates R. Aman's help with this article.

# POONERISMS

(Richard Christopher)

Most of us know somebody who occasionally says *revelant* for *relevant*, *pasghetti* for *spaghetti*, or *aminal* for *animal*. In each of these mispronunciations there is a switching of sounds between the two words; the scientific name for this phenomenon is *metathesis*, from the Greek meaning 'transpose'.

In English we call the intentional or unintentional transposition of letters, syllables, or words a *spoonerism*, named after the Revd William Archibald Spooner (1844–1930), once Warden of New College, Oxford. Spooner is said to have set out to become a *bird watcher* and instead to have ended up as a *word botcher*.

The first of Spooner's spoonerisms, and one of the few that have been authenticated, was spoken by the great man in 1879, when he was conducting a service at the College and announced the hymn as '*K*inkering *K*ongs Their Titles Take'. Other switches attributed to Spooner (most of them spuriously) include: 'Three cheers for our *qu*eer old *d*ean!' (referring to Queen Victoria); 'Is it *k*istomary to *cu*ss the bride?'; 'Stop *h*issing all my *m*ystery lectures'; 'You are occu*pew*ing my *pie*'; and 'The Lord is a *Sh*oving Leopard.'

Spoonerisms have become a prolific source of folk humour, but what has seldom been noted or explored is the fact that spoonerisms play a major role in the formation of bawdy jokes, a phenomenon that would have little pleased the good Reverend. For what I hope are obvious reasons, I would call such bawdy transpositions *poonerisms*. Here is a sampling of my favourites:

What's the difference between a pickpocket and a peeping Tom?
– *One snatches watches; the other watches snatches.* (Word transfer)

What's the difference between a nun at vespers and a nun in the bathtub?
– *One has hope in her soul, the other soap in her hole.* (Letter transfer)

What's the difference between a magician and a chorus line?
– *The magician has a c*unning array of *st*unts . . . (Letter transfer)

What's the difference between pigmies and female track stars?
– *Pigmies are cunning runts* . . . (Letter transfer)

What's the difference between an epileptic oysterman and a whore with diarrhoea?
– *One shucks between fits* . . . (Letter transfer)

Definition of a pimp: a snatch purser. (Syllable transfer)

Prostitute to customer: 'It's been a business doing pleasure with you.' (Word transfer)

A midget was fired from the circus for sticking his nose in everybody's business. A tall man was fired from the circus for sticking his business in everybody's nose. (Word transfer)

Radio blooper: 'Good evening, ladies and gentlemen, and welcome to another evening with the Canadian Broadcorping Castration.' (Syllable transfer)

The son of a shah is called a shan. A certain shan was afflicted with epilepsy. One day, the shan, moving amongst his harem, was smitten with a seizure. When his attendants arrived shortly thereafter, the harem girls inquired of them: 'Where were you when the fit hit the shan?' (Letter transfer)

## And, finally, the classic set-up poonerism:

A hunter was out shooting game in the wilds of Africa. When he came to a certain part of the jungle, all of his native bearers bolted in panic, save one – his most faithful companion. When the hunter asked the remaining bearer why the others had fled, he replied: 'You are about to enter the territory of the Great and Terrible Foo Bird. The Foo Bird has sixty-four teeth and a hundred-foot wingspan, but the worst thing is that, if you step on his turf, he will shit on your head. And if you wipe it off, you die.'

'Bosh,' replied the hunter, and took another step. Immediately the sky darkened as the Great and Terrible Foo Bird swooped down and planted a huge turd on the hunter's head.

Afraid to wipe off the Foo Bird pat that now sat upon his head, the hunter lived with it for five years. But it stank horribly and had an incredibly long half-life. Finally, the hunter could stand the stench no longer and proceeded to wipe off the turd.

And his head fell off, and he died.

**Moral:** *If the Foo shits, wear it.* (Letter transfer)

---

What is Jewish foreplay?
– *Two hours of begging.*

How does a French girl hold her liquor?
– *By the ears.*

Why did the West Germans elect a new chancellor?
– *Because they were tired of the same old Schmidt.*

What's the difference between a vulture and a Jewish mother?
– *The vulture waits until you're dead before it eats your heart out.*

How can you tell when a Jewish American Princess has an orgasm?
– *She drops her nail file.*

What's black and white and has a dirty name?
– *Sister Mary Elizabeth Fuck.*

# WHAT'S YOUR SIGN, SUCKER?

(Zack Isović)

**ARIES** (March 21 – April 19): You are the pioneer type and hold most people in contempt. You are quick-tempered, impatient and scornful of advice. You are not very nice.

**TAURUS** (April 20 – May 20): You are practical and persistent. You have a dogged determination and work like hell. Most people think you are stubborn and bull-headed. You are a Communist.

**GEMINI** (May 21 – June 20): You are a quick and intelligent thinker. People like you because you are bisexual. However, you are inclined to expect too much for too little. This means you are cheap. Geminis are known for committing incest.

**CANCER** (June 21 – July 22): You are sympathetic and understanding about other people's problems. They think you are a sucker. You are always putting things off. That's why you'll never make anything of yourself. Most welfare recipients are Cancer people.

**LEO** (July 23 – Aug. 22): You consider yourself a born leader. Others think you are pushy. Most Leo people are bullies. You are vain and dislike honest criticism. Your arrogance is disgusting. Leo people are thieves.

**VIRGO** (Aug. 23 – Sept. 22): You are the logical type and hate disorder. This nit-picking is sickening to your friends. You are cold and unemotional and sometimes fall asleep while making love. Virgos make good bus drivers.

**LIBRA** (Sept. 23 – Oct. 22): You are the artistic type and have a difficult time with reading. If you are a man you are more than likely queer. Chances for employment and monetary gains are excellent. Most Libra women are good prostitutes. All Libras die of venereal disease.

**SCORPIO** (Oct. 23 – Nov. 21): You are shrewd in business and cannot be trusted. You will achieve the pinnacle of success because of your total lack of ethics. Most Scorpio people are murdered.

**SAGITTARIUS** (Nov. 22 – Dec. 21): You are optimistic and enthusiastic. You have a reckless tendency to rely on luck, since you lack talent. The majority of Sagittarians are drunks or dope fiends. People laugh at you a great deal.

**CAPRICORN** (Dec. 22 – Jan. 19): You are conservative and afraid of taking risks. You don't do much of anything and are lazy. There has never been a Capricorn of any importance.

Capricorns should avoid standing still for too long, as they take root and become trees.

**AQUARIUS** (Jan. 20 – Feb. 18): You have an inventive mind and are jealous and possessive. You lie a great deal. On the other hand, you are inclined to be reckless and impractical; therefore you make the same mistakes over and over again. People think you are stupid.

**PISCES** (Feb. 19 – Mar. 20): You have a vivid imagination and often think you are being followed by the CIA or MI6. You have minor influence over your associates, and people resent you for flaunting your power. You lack confidence and are generally a coward. Pisces do terrible things to small animals.

---

Did you hear about the gay rabbi?
– *He kept blowing his shofar.*

What does a French-Chinese prostitute do?
– *She sucks your laundry.*

What do you call an overweight Chinese?
– *Chunk.*

Why don't Frenchmen eat flies?
– *Because they can't get their little legs apart.*

Why can't Santa Claus have any children?
– *Because he comes only once a year, and that's down the chimney.*

Have you heard about the gay burglar?
– *He couldn't blow the safe, so he went down on the elevator.*

# POSTMATURE ORGASTRIX

(Reinhold Aman)

According to female and quasi-male academics, male-oriented language has been a major reason for the inequality of women, keeping them with this tool in an inferior position (not to be confused with the Missionary Position). For instance, we have *spinster* but no equivalent for 'unmarried older man'. We can now do something about this inequality by creating terminology of female equivalents hitherto ignored by the chauvinist oinkers. Unlike their opponents, those shifty-eyed males suffering from sexual identity problems who mouth support for women's equality – thereby hoping for a grateful lay from fierce and frustrated feminists – I don't just pay lip service, as it were, to genuine equality. For example, elsewhere in this volume I have coined *clit-cheese*, the female equivalent of the male's *prick-cheese*.

In this excursion to sexolinguistics, seven new terms will be introduced to provide exact, scientific labels for the eight possible situations encountered in sexual intercourse. Equal attention has been given to the male and the female. Now, at last, the most glaring lacuna, the female equivalent of the male 'premature ejaculation', has been filled.

Premature ejaculation of the male occurs before the 'proper' or 'normal' time. This is, of course, a very subjective but commonly held notion. The man's timing may well be 'proper' or 'normal' but is 'too early' only in relation to the length of the woman reaching her orgasm. If it takes the female sex-partner 30 minutes or more to reach an orgasm, most ejaculations would have to be labeled 'premature'. The man's alleged premature ejaculation is belittled and has a *terminus technicus*, whereas the woman's slowness in reaching an orgasm is accepted as 'standard' or 'normal' and thus lacks a pejorative label.

The term *praecox* is derived from Latin *prae* ('before, early') and *coquere* ('to cook'), thus meaning 'ripe/done before its time'.

Note the seven holes, or gaps, in our language grid: we have no term for the female equivalent, nor any terms for orgasm occurring *at* the correct time, *after* the correct time, or *not at all*:

|       |                          | M | F |
|-------|--------------------------|---|---|
| pre-  | *before* the correct time | + | – |
| —     | at the correct time      | – | – |
| post- | *after* the correct time  | – | – |
| im-   | at *no* time             | – | – |

Thus, to fill these gaps in our linguistic pattern, I should like to propose the following complementary terminology for all possible situations; note that here 'ejaculation' refers to male orgasm, and 'climax' to female orgasm:

# MAN

**premature ejaculation** (*ejaculatio praecox*): ejaculation by the male *before* the woman reaches an orgasm (climax). Our standard, and only, term. Woman's most common reason for lamenting.

**mature ejaculation** (*ejaculatio cox*): ejaculation by the male *during* or shortly after the woman's climax. A normal woman's dream.

**postmature ejaculation** (*ejaculatio postcox*): ejaculation by the male long *after* the woman's climax. Relatively uncommon. A horny woman's dream.

**immature ejaculation** (*ejaculatio noncox*): non-occurrence of ejaculation by the male. Not to be confused with *impotence*.

# WOMAN

**premature orgasm** (*climax praecox*): orgasm by the woman *before* the man ejaculates. Every man's dream. Very rare.

**mature orgasm** (*climax cox*): orgasm by the woman *at the same time* the male ejaculates. A staple fantasy of erotic and pornographic writings and movies. Extremely rare in real life and – like the long-dicked dorks of porno movies – the cause of much male anxiety and sexual dysfunction.

**postmature orgasm** (*climax postcox*): orgasm by the woman long *after* the male has ejaculated and turned flaccid. The most common situation, especially in married couples, and a major cause why males go a-philandering, hoping to find the rare Premature Orgastrix.

**immature orgasm** (*climax noncox*): non-occurrence of orgasm by the female. Not to be confused with *frigidity*.

With these seven new, scientifically correct terms, we have not only filled linguistic gaps but have also provided the much-needed medical terminology to classify real-life situations, hitherto neglected by all sexual researchers.

When a male is blamed for 'premature' ejaculation, he can now counter the attack by accusing his female partner of 'postmature' orgasm, thus projecting his uncalled-for guilt-feelings on to her. However, rather than trading sexual insults, such as 'You postmature orgastrix!' or 'You're just a postmature orgasmette!', one would lead a healthier sex-life if one delayed or sped up one's orgasm. Those prone to 'postmature' orgasms can reach orgasm quickly by fantasizing about indecent acts with sheep or doorknobs, while their 'premature' counterparts can delay their orgasms by thinking of such chilling sex-partners as Margaret Thatcher or Henry Kissinger.

# THE SEX LIFE OF MICRO AND MILLIE

(Anon)

One night when his charge was exceptionally high, Micro Farad decided to seek out a cute little coil to let him discharge.

He picked up Millie Amp and took her for a ride on his megacycle. They rode across the Wheatstone bridge by the sine waves, and stopped in a magnetic field by a flowing current.

Micro Farad, attracted by Millie Amp's characteristic curves, soon was fully charged and had his field excited. He had her resistance to a minimum. He laid her on a ground potential, raised her frequency and lowered her capacitance.

He pulled out his high voltage probe, inserted it in her socket, connecting them in parallel, and began short-circuiting her resistance shunt. Fully excited, Millie mumbled, 'MHO, MHO, give me MHO.'

With his tube operating at a maximum peak, and her field vibrating with his current flow, Millie Amp soon reached her saturation point. The excessive current flow caused her shunt to overheat, and Micro Farad rapidly discharged and drained every electron.

They fluxed all night, trying various connections and sockets until his magnet had a soft core and lost all its field strength.

Afterwards, Millie Amp tried self-induction and damaged her solenoid. With his battery fully discharged, Micro Farad was unable to excite his generator. So they spent the rest of the night reversing polarity and blowing each other's fuse.

# SLOGANS TO PROMOTE NATIONAL CONDOM WEEK

(Reinhold Aman)

- Cover your stump before you hump
- Before you attack her, wrap your whacker
- Don't be silly, protect your willy
- When in doubt, shroud your spout
- Don't be a loner, cover your boner
- You can't go wrong if you shield your dong
- If you're not going to sack it, go home and whack it
- If you think she's spunky, cover your monkey
- It will be sweeter if you wrap your peter
- If you slip between the thighs, be sure to condomize
- She won't get sick if you wrap (cap) your dick
- If you go into heat, package (wrap) your meat
- While you are undressing Venus, dress up that penis
- When you take off her pants and blouse, suit up your trouser mouse
- Especially in December, gift-wrap your member
- Never (never) deck her with an unwrapped pecker
- Don't be a fool, vulcanize your tool
- The right selection? Check (sack) your erection
- Wrap in foil before checking her oil
- A crank with armour will never harm her
- Before you blast her, guard your bushmaster
- Before you bag her, sheath your dagger
- To save embarrassment later, cover your gator
- She'll be into fellatio, if you wrap your Horatio
- There's still cunnilingus with a shielded dingus, but she'll pass on fellatio if you've wrapped up Horatio

- Befo' da van start rockin', be sho' yo' cock gots a stockin'
- Before you let it all hang out, be sure to wrap your trouser
  trout
- Before you bang her, engulf your wanger
- Encase your porker before you dork her
- If you really love her, wear a cover
- Don't make a mistake, muzzle your snake
- Sex is cleaner with a package wiener
- If you can't shield your rocket, leave it in your pocket

From Germany comes:

\* *Nur ein Dummi macht ohne Gummi*
Only a dummy does (it) without (a) rubber

And, finally, some contributions from Newfoundland:

- No glove, not love
- Urge for a f\*\*k, reach for a latex
- When in doubt, leave it out
- Want to activate the cock, put on the sock
- When you are in charge, collect your discharge
- When there is a flutter in your pants, get the rubber in your
  hands

---

Why can't you circumcise Iranians?
– *Because there is no end to those pricks.*

Why do women rub their eyes when they get up in the
morning?
– *Because they have no balls to scratch.*

What is five miles long, forty feet wide, and has a collective IQ
of 35?
– *The St Patrick's Day Parade.*

# LIGHTBULB JOKES
## VARIATIONS ON A THEME

**How many . . . does it take to change a lightbulb?**

**Americans:** Six. One to change the bulb, and five to file environmental impact statements. (Told by a Norwegian student)

**Americans:** One. (As told in Poland)

**Californians:** None. Californians screw in a hot tub. (A very clever twist!)

**Dominatrices:** 'None, you ugly, snivelling piece of shit – *you'll* do it after I finish flogging you!' (A dominatrix is the superior member of a Bondage & Domination couple)

**Gays:** Five. One to change the bulb and four to hold the chandelier.

**Jewish Princesses:** None. They might chip their fingernails.

**Law Students:** Five. One to hold the bulb and four to kick the ladder out from under him. (Also told of **Republicans**)

**Psychiatrists/Psychoanalysts:** Only one, but it takes a very long time, and the light has to *really* want to change. (Variant: really *want*)

**Puerto Ricans:** Three. One to change the bulb and two to hold the radio.

**Women's Libbers/Feminists:** Five. One to change the bulb and four to write a magazine article about it. (Variants: Ten; nine to write about it. – Six: One to do it, three to write articles for *Ms.* on it, and two to discuss it at the next women's group meeting)

**Yuppies:** Two. One to mix the cocktails and one to call the electrician.

# A TABOO-BOO WORD REVISITED

(Richard Christopher)

Those people who wouldn't say *shit* if they had a mouthful may be fascinated to discover the many colourful and striking ways that the word is used in everyday speech. Indeed, the daring metaphors and clever coinages that spring from the word *shit* attest to the fact that it far outshines *fuck*.

## I. Literal Uses

*Take a shit, shit pot, shit paper, shithouse, good shit*

## II. Figurative Uses

*Up Shit Creek without a paddle, the shit hit the fan, wish in one hand and shit in the other, crock of shit, built like a brick shithouse, a sad sack of shit*
Animal metaphors: *Shit* linked with animal names means 'I don't believe a word of it', as in *pig, buzzard, hen, owl, whale, turtle, rat, cat* and *bat shit*, as well as the ever-popular *horse-shit*. But *bullshit* remains the most favoured, probably because of the prodigious quantity of functional droppings associated with the beast. On payday *the eagle shits*

## III. Insults

*Shit on you!, eat shit!, go shit in your hat!, full of shit, tough shit, shit-head* (recall Lieutenant Scheisskopf in *Catch-22*), *you shit, little shit, stupid shit, dumb shit, simple shit, shit-heel; he don't know shit from Shinola, shit or get off the pot, chickenshit, that shit don't fetch, to be shit on, not worth diddly* (or *doodly*) *shit, don't know whether to shit or go blind,*

157

*he thinks his shit don't stink, he thinks he's King Shit, shit-eating grin*

## IV. Fear

*Scared shitless, scare the shit out of, shit green* (or *blue*), *shit bricks, shit bullets, shit little blue cookies, shit out of luck, almost shit in his pants* (or *breeches*), *on someone's shit-list, have a shit haemorrhage*

## V. Tangibles and Intangibles

**Drugs:** *Shit,* in reference to heroin and marijuana. **Cards:** *Who dealt this shit?* **Food:** *Shit on a shingle* (or *stick*), usually referring to chipped beef or ground meat on toast and often acronymed *SOS.* **Objects:** *Who put all this shit on my bed?* **Talk:** *Shoot the shit, shovel the shit, I shit you not, no shit.* **Stuffing:** *Beat, kick, stomp,* or *knock the shit out of.* **Mind:** *Get your shit together*

## VI. Grammatical Intensifiers and Interjections

*Can't swim* (*run,* etc) *for shit* (or *worth a shit*), *who the shit are you?, let's get the shit out of here, holy shit!, no shit!, oh, shit!,* and the ever-reliable *shit!*

---

What's the difference between a Jew and a canoe?
– *A canoe tips.*

What do gays call haemorrhoids?
– *Speed bumps.*

If little girls are made of sugar and spice and everything nice, why do they all taste like anchovies?

# AN AGEIST LEXICON

**act one's age:** *v.* to behave as suitable for
**agèd:** *n., adj.* contemporary euphemism for *old* or *elders*
**anachronism:** *n.* anything out of its proper time. Meaning extended to elders to indicate that this group of people is out of step with current society
**anecdotage:** *n.* garrulous old age or senility (used humorously)
**anile:** *adj.* of or like an old woman
**anility:** *n.* the state of being anile
**antediluvian:** *adj.* very old; antiquated; primitive
**back number:** *n.* an anachronistic old man
**bag:** *n.* an unattractive woman (slang)
**baldy:** *n.* a person whose age is evidenced by loss of hair
**bat:** *n.* an ugly or nagging woman; shrew
**battleaxe:** *n.* an overbearing woman; virago (slang)
**beldam(e):** *n.* an old woman, especially one who is loathsome or ugly
**biddy:** *n.* a garrulous old woman (slang)
**bottle-nose:** *n.* an alcoholic old man
**caducity:** *n.* the frailty of old age
**cantankerous:** *adj.* ill-tempered and quarrelsome; disagreeable; contrary
**codger:** *n.* an old man (informal)
**constipated:** *adj.* reference to a supposed chronic condition of elders
**convalescent centre:** *n.* a warehouse for elders (euphemism)
**coot:** *n.* a foolish old man
**crank:** *n.* a grouchy person; an eccentric

**cranky:** *adj.* ill-tempered, peevish; odd, eccentric

**crone:** *n.* a withered, witchlike old woman

**crotchety:** *adj.* capriciously stubborn or eccentric; perverse

**debility:** *n.* the state of abnormal bodily weakness; feebleness

**declining years:** *n.* old age (euphemism)

**decrepit:** *adj.* weakened by old age, illness, or hard use; broken down

**decrepitude:** *n.* the state of being decrepit; weakness, infirmity

**dirty old man:** *n.* lecherous aged male

**doddering:** *adj.* feeble-minded from age; senile

**DOM:** *n.* acronym for DIRTY OLD MAN

**dotage:** *n.* second childhood; senility

**dotard:** *n.* a senile person

**dote:** *v.* to be foolish or feeble-minded, especially as a result of senility

**eccentric:** *adj.* departing from or deviating from the conventional or established norm, model, or rule

**fart:** *n.* a mean, contemptible person (vulgar slang)

**feeble:** *adj.* lacking strength; weak; especially frail or infirm

**feeble-minded:** *adj.* mentally deficient; subnormal in intelligence; dull-witted; stupid; foolish

**flabby:** *adj.* lacking firmness; loose and yielding to the touch; lacking force or vitality; feeble; ineffectual

**fogy:** *n.* a person of old-fashioned habits and outmoded attitudes

**fogyish:** *adj.* having the attributes of a FOGY

**fogyism:** *n.* having the traits of a FOGY

**fool:** *n.* one who shows himself, by words or actions, to be deficient in judgement, sense, or understanding; a stupid or thoughtless person

**foolish:** *adj.* lacking good sense or judgement; silly

**fossil:** *n.* one who is outdated or antiquated, especially a person with outmoded ideas; a fogy

**frail:** *adj.* having a delicate constitution; physically weak; not robust

**fuddy-duddy:** *n.* one who is old-fashioned and fussy

**fussbudget:** *n.* a person who fusses over trifles

**fussy:** *adj.* given to fussing; easily upset; insistent upon petty matters or details; fastidious

**gaffer:** *n.* an old man or rustic

**galoot:** *n.* a clumsy, uncouth, or sloppily dressed person

**garrulous:** *adj.* habitually talkative; loquacious

**geezer:** *n.* an eccentric old man

**generation gap:** *n.* reference to supposed philosophical and ideological differences between young and old (divisive term)

**geriatric generation:** *n.* elders as a group (derisive)

**geriatric ghetto:** *n.* home for elders

**Geritol generation:** *n.* elders as a group (derisive). Geritol is a patent medicine marketed for this age group

**goat:** *n.* a lecherous man

**golden age:** *n.* a period when a nation or some wide field of endeavour reaches its height. Euphemism for OLD AGE

**goose:** *n.* a silly person, a simpleton

**granny (grannie):** *n.* a grandmother; an old woman; a fussy person

**greybeard:** *n.* an old man

**grimalkin:** *n.* a shrewish old woman

**grouch:** *n.* a habitually complaining or irritable person

**grouchy:** *adj.* inclined to grumbling and complaint; ill-humoured; peevish

**grump:** *n.* a cranky, complaining person

**grumpy:** *adj.* fretful and peevish; irritable; cranky

**hag:** *n.* an ugly, frightful old woman; termagant; crone; a witch, sorceress

**infirm:** *adj.* weak in body, especially from old age; feeble

**infirmity:** *n.* lack of power; bodily debilitation; frailty

**little old lady:** *n.* a negative term, suggestive of impotency and frailty

**maid:** *n.* a girl or unmarried woman; a virgin

**miser:** *n.* one who deprives himself of all but the barest essentials to hoard money. A greedy or avaricious person

**mummy:** *n.* any withered or shrunken body, living or dead, that resembles a mummy

**obsolete:** *adj.* no longer in use or in fashion

**old cornstalk:** *n.* an ineffectual old man

**old-fashioned:** *adj.* of a style or method formerly in vogue; outdated; antiquated; attached to or favouring methods, ideas or customs of an earlier time

**old fuck:** *n.* old man (vulgar slang)

**old guard:** *n.* reactionary, corrupt and aged politician

**oldster:** *n.* an old or elderly person (informal)

**old-timer:** *n.* one who has been a resident, member, or employee for a long time. Something that is very old or antiquated

**old wives' tale:** *n.* a bit of superstitious folklore

**outmoded:** *adj.* not in fashion. No longer usable or practical; obsolete

**overage:** *adj.* beyond the proper or required age

**over the hill:** *adj.* no longer useful or functional

**peevish:** *adj.* querulous; discontented; fretful; ill-tempered; contrary; fractious

**pop:** *n.* an older man (derisive)

**rambling:** *adj.* lengthy and desultory

**reprobate:** *n.* morally unprincipled, profligate

**rickety:** *adj.* feeble with age; infirm

**second childhood:** *n.* a period of foolish, childlike behaviour allegedly experienced by the elderly

**senile:** *adj.* pertaining to, characteristic of, or proceeding from old age; exhibiting senility

**senile dementia:** *n.* progressive, abnormally accelerated deterioration of mental faculties and emotional stability in old age

**senility:** *n.* the state of being senile; mental and physical deterioration with old age

**senior citizen:** *n.* a person of or over the age of retirement

**show one's age:** *v.* to have the physical appearance of an elder person; to act the way society expects a person to act at a given age

**silly:** *adj.* showing lack of good sense; unreasoning; stupid

**spinster:** *n.* a woman who has remained single beyond the conventional age for marrying

**superannuated:** *adj.* retired or discharged because of age or infirmity; persisting ineffectively despite advanced age

**toothless:** *adj.* lacking teeth; lacking force; ineffectual
**trot:** *n.* an old woman (archaic)
**twilight years:** *n.* old age (euphemism)
**witch:** *n.* an ugly, vicious old woman; hag
**withered:** *adj.* dried up or shrivelled up as if from loss of moisture; lacking in freshness; faded; droopy
**wizen:** *adj.* shrivelled or dried up
**wizened:** *adj.* shrivelled, wizen
**wrinkled:** *adj.* drawn up; puckered

––––––––––––––

Three proofs that Christ was a Puerto Rican:
– *(1) His first name was Jesus; (2) He was always in trouble with the law; (3) His mother didn't know who His father was.*

Three proofs that Jesus was black:
– *(1) He called everybody 'brother': (2) He had no permanent address; (3) Nobody would hire him.*

Three proofs that Jesus was a Californian:
– *(1) He never cut his hair; (2) He walked around barefoot; (3) He founded a new religion.*

Three proofs that Jesus was an Italian:
– *(1) He talked with His hands; (2) He had wine at every meal; (3) He worked in the building trades.*

# POTENTIATION OF A SPANISH INSULT

(Mario E Teruggi)

*Hijo de puta*, 'son of a whore', is undoubtedly the most common personal insult in Spanish, and it is found in the classical literature of Spain as the contracted form *hideputa*. Of course, the formula is found in other languages, either straight or edulcorated, like *son of a bitch*, *son of a gun* and similar expressions in English.

In *hijo de puta* the emphasis is placed on the person whose mother is accused of having been a harlot; but, very often, the interest is displaced towards the mother herself, and the insulting formula is changed to *la puta que te parió*, 'the whore that bore you'. The English translation is very weak because there is no satisfactory equivalent of *parir*, since 'to bear, to give birth, to foal' or 'to calve' all lack the force and feeling of rudeness of the Spanish verb.

*La puta que te parió*, at least in Argentina, is now more frequently heard than *hijo de puta*. With the minor change of the dative pronoun *te* for the neuter *lo* (*la puta que lo parió*), it has an everyday use to discharge one's wrath, annoyance or ill humour against all sorts of inanimate objects, minor accidents or difficulties that stand in our way. The sentence is often reduced to a mere ¡*Que lo parió!* which is also employed to denote surprise or astonishment.

The frequent use of *la puta que lo parió* has, pebble-like, reduced much of its aggressiveness by the rounding off of its cutting edges and corners. That is the reason why, when we are really mad at somebody, we resort to two insults in order to give full vent to our indignation, saying in the same breath *¡Hijo de puta y la puta que te parió!* It is to be observed that the equivalents of *motherfucker* and *motherfucking* are not used in Spanish, although they would be perfectly understood and can be heard in Mexico (*¡Chinga tu madre!*, etc.).

Luckily for the people who want or need to utter their verbal aggressions with superlative strength, the Spanish language offers the possibility of raising the insult to a higher power, so to speak. In Argentina the maximum reinforcement is found in the utterance *¡La reputísima madre que te recontra mil parió!* which requires some explaining.

The prefix *re-*, as in English and many other languages, is used in Spanish to imply repetition or duplication. *Putísima* is the superlative of *puta*, here used as an adjective to be translated as 'most whorish'. *La reputísima madre* then means 'twice the (your) most whorish mother'. As to *recontra*, it means 'twice against' (*you* is implied) and is commonly used as a reply to an insult by simply muttering *que te recontra*, connoting 'the same to you but twice'. In the insult we are here considering, as a final reinforcement, the noun *mil*, 'one thousand', is added to *recontra*.

Thus, the whole sentence can be translated: 'The twice most whorish mother that bore you again and again one thousand times!'

In a mathematical approximation, if **W** stands for 'whorish' and **B** for 'bore,' the insult formula would be:

$$\text{Insult} = 2 \times W^2 \text{ mother} \ldots B\,(1 + 1) \times (1000)$$

Actually, $(1 + 1) \times (1000)$ is not understood in the sense that the mother gave birth 2000 times to the same child but as a definite reinforcement of the mother's whorishness.

In a nutshell: the mother that bore you was twice 2000 times squared a whore.

One wonders if other tongues have this possibility of numerically increasing common insults. Of course, one could simply say, 'Your mother was a billion times a whore', but it is the multiplying, doubling and squaring that, in a long crescendo, fills the utterer's mouth with a resounding and cathartic sonority.

---

A 'residential complex' developer in Spain's **Peñiscola**, Vinaroz, urges us to move there. (Advertisement in *L'Express*, Paris, 1 Nov. 1980, p. 57) – *I'll drink to that!* Ed.

Have you heard about the bloke who didn't know the difference between arson and incest?
– *He set fire to his sister.*

Why does Helen Keller masturbate with only one hand?
– *Because she needs the other one to moan.*

What is the best way to eat a frog?
– *Put a little leg over either ear.*

What weighs 18 stone and swims in the Thames estuary?
– *Moby Dyke.*

# TOM, DICK, AND HAIRY: MORE NOTES ON GENITAL PET NAMES

(Martha Cornog)

I am sitting in a room with about thirty women. We are all attending a session on 'vaginal consciousness raising' at a conference entitled 'A View Through the Speculum'. The session leader, a beautiful, vibrant woman of a 'certain age', asks us each to give the word(s) we use for our own genitals. 'Vagina' – 'Pussy' – 'Pussy Vagina' – 'Cunt' – 'Mama's box' – 'Henrietta'.

Some people, like the last two women, use pet names to refer to their genitals. In *Lady Chatterley's Lover*, the fictional Mellors calls his penis 'John Thomas' and Constance Chatterley's vulva 'Lady Jane'. Names like these (*Mama's Box, Henrietta, John Thomas*) I call genital pet names. They function as proper names and refer to an individual's genitals only. In this way, they differ from general slang terms for genitals (eg, *pussy, bearded clam, box, dick, cock, hog, one-eyed wonder worm*) because they are personal, proper names.

Not only fictional characters like Mellors use pet names: real people name their genitals, too. To date, I have collected over thirty such pet names.

The information given with each pet name follows this pattern (where supplied): significance or meaning of name; circumstances of naming or 'christening'; the age of the owner of the genital at the time the name was used; and location.

## PET NAMES FOR THE PENIS

**Alice:** 'Put Alice in Wonderland'. From Lewis Carroll's book. See **Wonderland**. Private language between lovers

**Baby:** 'Does Baby want to go Home?' See **Home**. Private language between lovers. Age 20. Indiana

**Broom:** Couple undergoing marriage counselling (see text, below). Indiana

**Casey:** After Casey Jones, the brave engineer, who took a trip 'into the promised land'. Private language between lovers. Named by the woman. Age 20. Rhode Island

**Chuck:** Middle name of owner. Private language between lovers. Named by the woman during sex play. Age 33. Ohio

**Dipstick:** Couple undergoing marriage counselling. Indiana

**Driveshaft:** Couple undergoing marriage counselling. Indiana

**Four on the Floor:** A car's gearshift. Couple undergoing marriage counselling. Indiana

**Gearstick:** Couple undergoing marriage counselling. Indiana

**George:** 'Let George do it.' Age 24. Pennsylvania

**Gnarled Tree Trunk** (GTT for short): Shape of penis (heavily veined). Private language between lovers. Named by the woman during sex play. Age 50. Pennsylvania

**Hank:** Named by owner at male drinking party (see text, below). Age 60. Pennsylvania

**Jason:** London, England

**Jawillbemy:** Possibly a shortening of 'Jane will be my . . . ' Private language of flirtation (couple were not lovers). Age 18. Oklahoma

**Lazarus:** 'He rises from the dead.' Age 33. Washington, DC

**Little Weese:** 'Weese' is a Midwestern mispronunciation of owner's surname. Private language within intimate network of three couples. Age 20. Ohio

**Little Willy:** Owner named Bill. 'Little' is ironic, as 'Little Willy' is nine inches long, according to Bill's ex-wife

**Mortimer:** Private language between lovers. Named by the woman during sex play. Age 28. Ohio. See **Eunice,** below

**Periwinkle:** Private language between lovers. May have been used previously by the man

**Peter J Firestone:** 'Peter' from common slang for penis, 'J Firestone' from middle initial and last name of owner. Private language between lovers. Age 18. Ohio

**Putz:** Yiddish for 'penis'. Private language within intimate network of three couples. Age 20. Ohio

**Sniffles:** Man had slight genital discharge; doctor suggested that maybe he had 'caught a cold'. Private language between lovers. Age 20. Toronto, Canada. Man (informant) is originally from the UK

**Winston:** 'Tastes good, like a cigarette should.' Private language between lovers. Age 30. Pennsylvania

**Zeke:** Private language within intimate network of three couples. Age 20. Ohio

## PET NAMES FOR THE VULVA

**Eunice:** Old-fashioned name, corresponding to **Mortimer** (see above). Private language between lovers. Named by the man during sex play. Ohio

**Henrietta:** Pennsylvania

**Home:** 'Does Baby want to go Home?' See **Baby.** Private language between lovers. Age 20. Indiana

**Little Monkey:** 'Can I pet the Little Monkey?' Couple undergoing marriage counselling. Indiana

**Mama's Box:** Age 35. Pennsylvania.

**Rochester:** From the city where she lost her virginity. Private language within intimate network of three couples. Age 20. Ohio

**Virginia Vagina:** Alliteration. Private language within intimate network of three couples. Age 20. Ohio

**Wonderland:** 'Put Alice in Wonderland.' See **Alice.** Private language between lovers

Although this list of names is not long, we can discern some patterns of naming, particularly for the penis. Most names of penises fall into one of the following categories:

1. A variation of the owner's name (*Little Willy*, *Chuck*,

*Peter J Firestone*). 2. A name suggesting a joke or catchy phrase, usually alluding to erection or sex acts (*Lazarus, Winston*). 3. What Sanders and Robinson call 'power slang' (*Driveshaft, Four on the Floor*). 4. Human first names that appealed or occurred to the namer for no reason that could be recalled by the informant. 'The Saturday night of Opening Day [of trout season] I can remember vividly. [My father] he was drunker than a warthog . . . We get out on the porch [to urinate] and he's . . . singing "I took my organ to the party", . . . he gets his fly open . . . and he starts to relieve himself – a fairly steady stream – and he starts talking to his organ and, by God, he calls the thing "Hank". He says, "Aw, look at old Hank here, poor, poor old guy." And he says, "You and I, we've been in a couple of tight places together and we've had our ups and downs, but I want you to know, you old sonofabitch" – and this is where he starts shaking it off – "that I outlived you!" . . . That was the first time I had heard him allude to "Hank" [and] I think it was just a spur-of-the-moment thing.'

Some of the same patterns occur among the names for vulvas (*Wonderland*, for example). However, I have collected too few names for vulvas to be able to generalize at this point.

Who names genitals? In those cases where I was told the full story by the informant of the 'christening' (16 cases out of 33), it was most often a group or couple interaction, or the other partner who produced the name. (For the remaining cases, this information was not available.) Penises seem to be named more often than vulvas.

Why do some people give proper names to genitals? After all, no one names feet, hands or elbows. Genital proper or pet names serve one or more functions.

First, the name(s) can serve as a private language between lovers or other groups of people who know each other well. Such a language permits discussion of sexual matters in front of unknowing friends and parents. The woman who told me about *Peter J Firestone* said, 'We would be sitting at dinner [with his parents] and he would toss off this comment, "Well, maybe we could double-date with Peter tonight," and then we'd go, "Ha, ha, ha," and hope that his mother didn't see me turn red!' Similarly, the owner of *Winston* and his girlfriend took great pleasure in discussing 'Winston's good taste' in front of friends and relatives. One sex manual advises genital naming for this purpose:

> Pat your man's penis during nonsexual moments. Give it a pet name such as 'John Thomas' used by Lawrence's Lady Chatterley; or name it after its owner, calling it 'Junior' – 'David, Junior', 'Mark, Junior', etc. A girl I know has long hilarious conversations with someone named Penis Desmond – P D, for short – who answers her in a high-pitched falsetto voice. This little act is a fun way to humanize a woman's relationship to a man's penis. [Note that here the woman partner is advised to do the naming, and to pick a variation of the owner's name.]

In a broader sense, the pet name can also serve as a method of facilitating communication about sex. Many people, particularly women, are uncomfortable with the common generic terms for genitals. One of my informants was a marriage counsellor for several years:

> One of the things we frequently encountered were persons who were having a great deal of difficulty verbally communicating about sex, and the reason was that they were extremely . . . uncomfortable with what they considered to be profane words, and they were uncomfortable with the official Latin terminology. And what was typically going on, then, was just nothing. With lack of a label, people weren't talking. So . . . after playing around with it for a while, I thought about the possibility of using made-up words. So we started doing that in therapy [having the couples make up names for body parts and sex acts] and we found it to be very successful. A lot of couples who had had trouble before really got into it, found it very enjoyable and developed a whole new vocabulary for sex organs and sexual acts . . . From a therapeutic point of view, it was a very good idea, because, in addition to giving them a label that they could use to communicate and increase the effectiveness of what they were doing . . . it [also] created a very nice thing for them to do together. The process of thinking up names and developing this new vocabulary was a very enjoyable process of sharing for most of the couples that tried it.

Finally, the pet name bestows an identity upon the genitals: they have a personality which *is distinct* from the identity of the owner:

The experience of genital excitation parallels the experience of the I in that it has a somewhat detached quality . . . In men the penis is often given a name to indicate that it has a degree of independence from the self. It may be called 'John', or *le petit homme* [the little man], or 'Peter', to denote this independence from the self.

Much current popular literature on sex and psychology describes the alienation and the love/hate relationship men often have with their penises: ' . . . He curses his penis for not performing, as he sweats and strains and informs his partner that *he* really wants to, even though something is wrong with *it*.' And Jerry Rubin gives the dialogue:

> *My penis*: I don't want to get turned on here. This bed is not safe for me.
> *My mind*: Shut up! Perform! Don't let me down! . . . You're humiliating me in front of Rosalie!

A man having some of these feelings who gives a pet name to his penis can thereby both wash his hands of what 'it' does and also diffuse his anxiety through humour. Lawrence's Mellors illustrates this process:

> The man [Mellors] looked down in silence at the tense phallos, that did not change. – 'Ay!' he said at last, in a little voice, 'Ay ma lad! tha'art thee right enough. Yi, the mun rear thy head! Theer on thy own, eh? an' ta'es no count o'nob'dy! Tha ma'es nowt o' me, John Thomas. Art boss? of me? Eh well, tha'rt more cocky than me, an' that says less. John Thomas! Dost want *her*? Dost want my lady Jane? . . . Tell Lady Jane tha wants cunt, John Thomas . . . '

Thus, we have the theme of genitals-as-personality. We can also call this 'genitomorphism.' It goes much further than the practice of giving proper names to genitals. It reaches into psychology, folklore, literature, art and religion. Included in this theme of genitomorphism are the subthemes of talking genitals, genitals talked to and genitals acting on their own volition. Finally, of course, we have Genital Gods, ie, phallic worship. Above, I have noted some of the psychological correlates of naming genitals. Gershon Legman discusses the folklore of genitomorphism in his *Rationale of the Dirty Joke* (First and Second Series). He provides nearly twenty jokes or tales dealing with genitals named, speaking, spoken to, or acting on their own. Several examples, condensed here:

1. Groom on honeymoon to bride: 'Honey, would you like to see *Oliver Twist?*'
Bride: 'Why not? I've seen it do everything else!'
2. Prostitute sees reflection of her vulva in a puddle: 'There you is, you l'il ol' money-maker!'
3. Man amputates penis accidentally while shaving. Severed penis: 'I know we've had lots of fist fights in our time, but I never thought you'd pull a knife on me!'

And a wonderful cartoon was described to me of a man holding his penis, which is saying (via a cartoon 'balloon'), 'Not tonight, dear, I have a headache!'

In literature, I have already mentioned *Lady Chatterley's Lover*, but I have found other interesting examples. In *Portnoy's Complaint*, Portnoy has a long dialogue with 'the maniac who speaks into the microphone of my jockey shorts'. Henry Miller, in *Tropic of Capricorn*, gives a long and detailed typology of 'cunt personalities'. The hero of Petronius's *Satyricon*, Encolpius, has a violent argument with 'a part of me which no serious man thinks worthy of his thoughts'.

In the graphic arts, genitals have been depicted as self-contained beings, or as the heads of otherwise human bodies. Fourteen plates in *The Complete Book of Erotic Art* depict this theme, including a delightful series of Japanese prints of a Sumo wrestling match between a penis and a vulva, which ends (not surprisingly) with the penis being engulfed by the vulva/vagina.

Finally, a substantial literature concerns phallic worship. Edwardes gives one example in *The Jewel in the Lotus*, where he describes 'the evil *jinee El-A'awer* [one-eyed penis genie], patron spirit of the ravisher.'

Genitals named, genitals spoken to, genitals acting independently, and genitals deified are related themes. All are subsumed under the broader concept of 'genitals-as- personality.' But we have yet to understand fully why genitals are personified, the cultural conditions under which personification happens, and, finally, what it means to people who say *Henrietta* or *Winston* to genitals.

———————————

What's the difference between a new bride and a new job?
– *After six months, the new job still sucks.*

When does a cub scout become a boy scout?
– *After he eats his first Brownie.*

What's the difference between a Sloane Ranger and a bowling ball?
– *You can only get three fingers into a bowling ball.*

What goes 'ha-ha-ha-ha THUMP'?
– *A leper laughing his head off.*

# TALK DIRTY TO ME . . . JUST ONCE MORE: SEXY SLOGANS

(Reinhold Aman)

**Nice . . .**

A dirty mind is a terrible thing to waste
A morner is like a nooner, only sooner
Beware of religions that have waterslides
Can I do it 'til I need glasses?
Chaste makes waste
Chastity is its own punishment
It was hard when I kissed her goodbye
Lie down, I think I love you
O Lord, help me to be pure, but not yet
Polymer physicists are into chains
Running is an unnatural act, except from the enemy and to the
    bathroom
Sex is not the answer; sex is the question. 'Yes' is the answer

**Nasty . . .**

Do you fuck, suck, swallow & take it up the ass – or am I
    wasting my time on a Jesus Freak?
Fuck the Real World – I'm an Artist
I had better sex in prison
I make money the old-fashioned way. I'm a whore
I peed on Santa's lap
I'd like to give you what you deserve, but my dog's constipated
I'm not very smart, but I'm real good with zippers
I've got the time if you've got the kneepads

If we are what we eat, I could be you by morning
Intolerant self-righteous castrating bitch with PMS
It wasn't your brains that attracted me, so shut the fuck up
Jesus loves you. Everyone else thinks you're an asshole
Men are such assholes
Mr Rogers: 'Can you say "Cunnilingus"?'
Pardon me, but you're standing on my penis
Show me a successful woman & I'll show you a frustrated bitch
Sure, I'm ugly. But, I can really fuck
Thank you for not jacking off on the furniture
Thank you for not smoking, spitting, bleeding, dropping scabs,
   or excreting any pus
The solution to your problem is in my pants
You have a nice face – but that fat ass has got to go

---

### PIT, TIT, CLIT

A young Midwest lady calls her lover, who attaches his mouth with the fierceness of a pit bull to her breasts and nipples, *tit-bull*. She also calls him *clit-bull*, as he is 'the best cunnilinguist west of Brest' who is down on his knees faster than a zealous monk and doesn't let go of her yummy labia minora and clitoris until she has reached at least three major orgasms. (Readers unsure of their knowledge of world geography are advised to consult a map of France and find Brest, a seaport located at the nipple of Brittany, which sticks out into the Atlantic Ocean like a firm breast.)

# IRANIAN VALUES AS DEPICTED IN FARSI TERMS OF ABUSE, CURSES, THREATS, AND EXCLAMATIONS

(Soraya Noland and D M Warren)

Farsi, the national language of Iran, belongs to the Indo-Iranian group of languages. It has been influenced by many different languages introduced to Iran over the past centuries by such migrant ethnic groups as the Mongols, Turks, Arabs, Greeks, Russians and, more recently, the Europeans. The numerous minority ethnic groups living in Iran, such as the Turks, Baluchis, Kurds, Bakhtiaris, Gilakis, and Arabs all speak their own languages, with Farsi learned as a second language through the public school system, as Farsi is the national language for instruction in schools. Non-Muslim religious minorities in Iran, such as the Armenians, Jews, Baha'is, and Zoroastrians are other distinct groups within Iran, although only the Armenians continue to speak their own language as a first language. Farsi is also spoken in Afghanistan, where it is referred to as Dari. The abusive terms listed in this article are used by the Farsi-speaking Muslims of Iran, although the very use of most of the terms is considered improper behaviour by the majority of Iranians.

Many of the Farsi abusive terms focus on the values of honour and prestige. The concepts of honour and modesty are well discussed by such authors as Abu-Zeid, Antoun, and Bourdieu. The honour of an individual may be stained through his or her act and/or through his relatives' (female and male) immodest behaviour. Furthermore, the role one assumes in the sexual act itself may be an issue of social dominance. In both heterosexual and homosexual relationships, the individual who assumes the 'male' role dominates the individual who assumes the 'female' role. The 'male' partner is superior in a social power sense to the 'female' partner. Therefore, an abuse which focuses upon having intercourse with the addressee's relatives is a statement of superiority by the abuser. As such, it is considered an insult to the addressee.

Abusive terms are usually used by individuals of a higher social status and/or by an older person in relation to the addressee. Individuals of the same age also exchange abusive terms. Unless otherwise stated in the following list, the terms may be used by both males and females to abuse either other males or females. However, an individual of a lower social status and/or a younger individual would rarely use such terms in a face-to-face situation with individuals either older or of higher social classes.

Another category of abusive terms consists of wishing one ill or dead. It is assumed, regardless of the age of the individual, that his/her parents are responsible for his/her shortcomings in terms of personality. Attributing animal qualities to individuals comprises another category of Farsi abusive terms; animals are considered inferior to human beings in Iranian culture, too.

Romanization of the Farsi terms in this article follows the English Transliteration System as published in the *International Journal of Middle East Studies*. The circumflex (^) is used in this glossary, instead of the customary diacritical mark indicating a long vowel, the macron (¯).

## PRONUNCIATION GUIDE

**ai** as in 'tail'; **ch** as in 'change'; **gh** has no English equivalent but sounds approximately like **g** in 'girl'; **h** as in 'hat'; **j** as in 'jam'; **kh** has no English equivalent but sounds approx. like Scottish 'loch'; **q** approx. like **qu** in 'quick'; **s** as in 'sand'; **sh** as in 'shower'; **th** is Arabic *th* but in Farsi sounds like **s** as in 'simple'; **v** as in 'vicious'; **w** in Arabic *uww* as in 'wound'; **u** as in 'road'; **y** as in 'ink'; glottal stop ' sounds approx. like Scottish *bo'l* 'bottle.'

# FARSI VERBAL ABUSE

## I Insults attacking physical deviations and shortcomings

(1) چشمت کور

**chishmit kûr**: 'may you become blind!'

(2) چلاق

**chulâgh**: 'arm': a clumsy person

(3) دندت نرم

**dandit narm**: 'may your ribs get crushed!'

(4) دراز بی عقل

**dirâz-i-bi-aghl**: 'tall and without brains'. Tall individuals are considered dumb

(5) فیل

**fîl**: 'elephant': a fat and stupid person. Fat persons are considered stupid

(6) گردن دراز

**gardan dirâz**: 'long neck': a clumsy person. Used for tall persons, it is a general reference to the camel which is considered clumsy

(7) خرس

**khirs**: 'bear': a fat and lazy person. Fat persons are considered lazy

(8) کس گنده

**kus gundih**: 'big cunt': a lazy woman. This term is used only against women

(9) کس گشاد

**kus qushâd**: 'wide/big cunt': a lazy woman. A term used only by and against women

(10) کس زنت

**kusi zanit**: 'your wife's cunt'. This term is used only by men

(11) کوتاه موذی

**kûtah-i-mûzy**: 'short and sneaky'. Short individuals are considered to possess a sneaky trait

(12) لنگ دراز

**ling dirâz**: 'long legs': a tall and insensitive individual. Tall individuals are considered insensitive

(13) مردنی

**murdanî**: 'you who look like you are dying': you weakling. Addressed to physically weak, feeble and pale-looking persons

(14) شمشیر از کون سگ درآمده

**shamshîr az kûn-i-sag dar âmadih**: 'a sword pulled out of a dog's ass': a feeble or pale-looking or skinny person

(15) شتر

**shutur**: 'camel': a tall and clumsy person

## II Insults attacking intellectual and mental deviations and shortcomings

(16) بوقلمون

**bû ghalamûn**: 'turkey': an unstable personality; a person who is ideologically unstable. The neck wattle of turkeys is considered to change colours; this term refers to persons who continually change their positions or attitudes

(17) دراز گوش

**dirâz gûsh**: 'long ears': a donkey; a stupid person

(18) گاو

**gâv**: 'cow': a stupid person; an insensitive person; one without manners

(19) کره خر

**kurih khar**: 'donkey's child': a stupid person. The donkey is a symbol of stupidity

(20) کسش خله

**kusish khulih**: 'her cunt is crazy': a stupid woman. Used by both men and women to abuse a woman

(21) تخم جن

**tukhmih jin**: 'testicles of the *jinn*': a clever but dishonest person. The *jinn* (supernatural beings, spirits, demons) are believed to have superior intelligence in the Iranian culture. The abuse also means that the person addressed is not the son of a human male, but rather the son of a *jinn*

## III Insults attacking individual and social deviations and shortcomings

(22) عقرب زیرتالی

**aghrab zîr ghâly**: 'scorpion under the rug': a sneaky person

(23) عوض زانیدن ریدی

**avazi zâidan rîdî**: 'you shat instead of giving birth': a hopeless person. This term is addressed to the mother of an individual who is considered incapable of doing anything correctly

(24) ازصدتا عقرب و مار بدترہ

**az sad tâ aghrab-u-mâr bad tarih**: 'worse than a hundred scorpions and snakes': a sneaky person

(25) بابات بکونت

**bâbât bi kûnit**: 'your father is in your ass!' A general abuse addressed to both men and women

(26) بد اصل

**bad asl**: 'evil nature': an evil man

(27) بد بخت

**bad bakht**: 'unfortunate': an unfortunate person

(28) باد دماغ

**bad-i-damagh**: 'wind in the nose': an arrogant person. The term refers to wind blowing into a person's nose, swelling up his or her head

(29) بی اصل و نسب

**bî asl-u-nasab**: 'without origin or title': a low-class person

(30) بی بند و بار

**bî band-u-bâr**: 'without any moral standards': an immoral person

(31) بیچاره.

**bî chârih:** 'without any choice': an unfortunate person

(32) بی چشم و رو.

**bî chishm-u-rû:** 'without eye and without face': a shameless
person

(33) بدماغ بابات ریدم

**bi damâghi bâbât rydam:** 'I shit on your father's nose!' A
general abuse addressed to both men and women

(34) بی حیا.

**bî hayâ:** 'shameless': a shameless person

(35) به جهنم

**bi jahanam:** 'go to hell!' A general abuse addressed to both
men and women

(36) بی سر و بی پا.

**bî sar-u-bî pâ:** 'without a head and without feet': a low-class
person; one without roots

(37) به کونش میگه با من نیا که بوت میاد

**bih kûnish mygih bâ man niâ ki bût myâd:** 'he/she tells his/her
ass, "do not come with me because you stink" ': an
arrogant person

(38) بمیر تا کسی نمرده

**bimyr tâ kasy na murdih:** 'die before anyone else does!': drop dead!

(39) بری که بر نگردی

**biry kih bar na gardy:** 'go somewhere so you won't return!':
get lost!

(40) چاک دهنت به بند

**châki dahanit biband:** 'shut your mouth!'

(41) چنان میزنم توی دهنت که سرت به عقب بر گرده

**chinan myzanam tûyi dahanat ki sarit bi aqab bar gardih:** 'I
will hit you in the mouth so hard that your head swings
back!': I'll knock your block off! This is a threat which
becomes an insult if used by someone of low status against
someone else of higher status or age

(42) چشم چرون

**chishm charûn:** 'grazing eyes'. Used against a male who stares at women too much

(43) چشم تنگ

**chishm tang:** 'narrow eyes': a greedy person

(44) چس خور

**chus khur:** 'fart-eater': a stingy person

(45) دهن لق

**dahan lagh:** 'loose mouth': one who can't keep a secret

(46) دست کج

**dast kaj:** 'crooked hand': a thief; a dishonest person

(47) دیوث

**dayuwwth:** 'pimp'

(48) فلک زده

**falak zadih:** 'being beaten by the world': an unfortunate or hopeless person

(49) گم شو

**gaum shu:** 'get lost'

(50) گدازاده

**gidâ zâdih:** 'son of a beggar/born of a beggar': a low-class and stingy person. Addressed to individuals from low status who are not generous.

(51) گه به گیست

**guh bi gîsit:** 'may shit be on your hair!' A term of disrespect used by males or females against women

(52) گه به گیس مادرت

**guh bih gîsih mâdarit:** 'may shit be on your mother's hair!': you worthless person!

(53) گه لوله

**guh lûlih:** 'rolled in shit': a worthless person

(54) گربه کوره

**gurbih kûrih:** 'blind cat': an ungrateful or unkind person

گوشت رون نمی حوره میگه مال در کونه (55)

**gûshti rûnih ni mykhurih mîgih mâlih dar kûnih:** 'he/she does not eat the rump roast because it is close to the ass': an arrogant person. *Kûn* is a single term in Farsi which is used to refer both to the anus and the buttocks

گوز به ریشت (56)

**gûz bi rîshit:** 'may a fart be on your beard!' A term of disrespect used by both males or females against men

هرجائی (57)

**har jâî:** 'sexually loose': a sexually loose woman. This term is milder than 'prostitute' and is used by women to refer to other women

حرام لقمه (58)

**harâm luqmih:** 'a person who eats stolen food': a dishonest person. *Harâm* is a term which refers to unclean or unlawful items or acts according to the teachings of Islam

حرام زاده (59)

**harâm zâdih:** 'bastard': a tricky or malicious person

جاکش (60)

**jâ kash:** 'pimp'

جونمرگ بشی اللهی (61)

**jûni marg bishî illahî:** 'may God kill you in your youth!' Addressed to young people. In Persian culture, wishing one to become old is a compliment

جونت دربره (62)

**jûnit dar birih:** 'may your life end!': I wish you were dead!

کم از عنش بخور (63)

**kam az anish bi khur:** 'don't eat his/her shit so much': a flatterer; a brown-noser

کم ازکونش به حور (64)

**kam az kûnish bi khur:** 'don't eat his ass!' Addressed to individuals who stick up for someone else too much

(65) کاش کمر بابات خشگ شده بود

**kâsh kamar bâbât khushg shudih bûd**: 'may that your father's back had been dried up!' This phrase is used in situations where it is wished that the addressee had not been born at all. In Persian culture, it is believed that semen originates in the back of a man's waist. The term 'back' refers only to the back portion of one's waist

(66) خبیث

**khabîth**: 'evil nature': an evil man

(67) خفقان بگیر

**khafiqân bigîr**: 'shut up!'

(68) خواهرت گائیدم

**khâharit gâîdam**: 'I fucked your sister.' This phrase is used only by men

(69) خاک بر سرت

**khâk bar sarit**: 'may soil/dirt be on your head!' This phrase is used when wishing someone dead or wishing someone's father dead. Dirt is put on the head as a sign of grief during the Persian funeral ceremony

(70) خدا تورا بکشد

**khodâ tu râ bikushad**: 'may God kill you!'

(71) کیرم به کس زنت

**kiîram bi kusi zanit**: 'my prick is in your wife's cunt!'

(72) کون گشاد

**kûn goshâd**: 'wide anus': a lazy person. A term addressed to both lazy men and lazy women

(73) کون گنده

**kûn gundih**: 'wide buttocks': a lazy person. A term addressed to both lazy men and women

(74) کون کلفت

**kûn kuluft**: 'big ass': a lazy person. A term addressed to both lazy men and women

كو نى (75)

**kûnî:** 'queer'. In Farsi, this term refers only to the male who assumes the female rôle in homosexual intercourse. Both males and females may use this term to abuse a male

كس كس (76)

**kus kash:** 'a person who trades in cunt': 'a cunt-trader', pimp

كيرم به كون خوابر مادرت (77)

**kyram bi kûni khâhar/mâdarit:** 'my prick is in your sister's/ mother's ass!'

كيرم توى دبنت (78)

**kyram tûyi dahanit:** 'my prick is in your mouth!'

لكا ته (79)

**lakâtih:** 'whore'

لنگ كفش كهنه (80)

**lingi kafsh kuhnih:** 'an old shoe': a person who stands up for somebody else too much

لنگت پاره مى كنم (81)

**lingit pârih mykunam:** 'I will tear your crotch apart!' A term used only between/among women

مادر سگ (82)

**mâdar sag:** 'your mother is a dog': a low-class person. In Iranian and Islamic culture, the dog is considered unclean

مادرت و خوابرت (83)

**mâdarit au khâharit:** 'your mother and your sister!' This is a shortened version of 'I fuck your mother and I fuck your sister!' Even the naming of the mother, sister, or wife by a man to another man is considered an insult in Iranian culture

مادرت بعزا يت به نشينه (84)

**mâdârit bi azâyat bishînih:** 'may your mother mourn for you!'

A phrase used by someone wishing that the addressee
were dead

مادرت می گام (85)

**mâdarit mygâm:** 'I fuck your mother!'

میمونه هرچه زشتتره بازیش بیشتره (86)

**maymûnih har chî zishtarih bâzîsh bîshtarih:** 'the uglier the
monkey the more active he/she is.' This phrase is used to
refer to individuals who are physically ugly or of low
social status but who behave arrogantly

مثل چُسه نه بو داره نه حاصیت (87)

**misli chusih – na bû darih na khâsiat:** 'just like a fart – it has
neither smell nor use': a useless person. The term *chusih*
in Farsi refers to soundless, odourless farts; the term *gûz*
refers to the type of fart which has both sound and
odour

مثل سنده که ازکون سگ بهکشی بیرون (88)

**misli sindih kih az kûni sag bi kashî bîrûn:** 'just like shit pulled
out of a dog's ass': a feeble person; a hopeless person

عمرت سربره (89)

**'mrit sar birih:** 'may your life end!': I wish you were dead!

موش مُرده (90)

**mûsh-i-murdih:** 'dead mouse': a sneaky individual

میزنم تُوی لنگت (91)

**myzanam tûyi lingit:** 'I will hit you in your crotch/cunt!' This
phrase is used only between/among women

میزنم تُوی مخت که بری زیرزمین (92)

**myzanam tûyi mukhit ki biry zîri zamyn:** 'I will punch your
brain so that you will be buried under the ground!' A
threat which can become an insult (*see* No. 41)

نفست بند بیاد (93)

**nafasit band birih:** 'may you stop breathing!': may you die!

قرتی (94)

**qirtî:** 'gigolo'

(95) پا بدر

**pâ bidar:** 'loose': a loafer

(96) پا کج

**pâ kaj:** 'crooked foot': a sexually loose woman

(97) پفیوز

**pufyûz:** 'pompous'. This term is addressed only to men

(98) ریدم بگور پدرت

**rîdam bi gûr-i-pidarat:** 'may shit be on your father's grave!'

(99) روح بابات سگ رید

**rûhi bâbât sag rîd:** 'may a dog shit on your father's grave!'

(100) سگ

**sag:** 'dog': a feisty or quarrelsome person

(101) سگ پدر

**sag pidar:** 'your father is a dog': a low-class person

(102) سلیطه

**salîtih:** 'loudmouth': a woman who brawls often and screams too much

(103) سرخز توی لنگت

**sari khar tûyi lingit:** 'a donkey's head is in your cunt': you dumb cunt. This term is used only between/among women

(104) شلخته

**shilakhtih:** 'messy person': a woman who does not take proper care of her children and household

(105) شل و ول

**shul-u-vil:** 'loose': an incapable person

(106) تخم حرام

**tukhmi harâm:** 'bastard': a dishonest person; literally, 'unclean semen *or* testes'. *Tukhmi* refers both to the testes and to semen; *harâm* means unclean in the religious, Islamic sense.

(107) توله سگ

**tûlih sag:** 'puppy': a low-class person

(108) وِلگرد

vilgard: 'loose': a man who meanders without apparent aim and who goes anywhere even without invitation; ie a man who acts as if none of society's norms applied to him

(109) وِلنگار

vilingâr: 'loose': a woman who exhibits loose (non-sexual) behaviour. The female equivalent of *vilgard* (*see* No. 108)

(110) زبان دراز

zabân dirâz: 'long tongue': an outspoken person

(111) زبان تیز

zabân tîz: 'sharp tongue'

(112) زبانت مار و عقرب گَبزِه

zabûnit mâr-u-aghrab bi gazih: 'may your tongue be bitten by a snake and a scorpion!' A phrase used in wishing the other dead or speechless

(113) زهرِ مار

zahri mâr: 'snake poison'. A term used in wishing one dead

(114) زهرِ مار هم نمیدم

zahri mâr ham nimydam: 'I don't even give snake poison.' A phrase which indicates that 'I would not give you anything'

(115) زنِ جنده / زنِ قحبه

zani jindih / zani qahbih: 'your wife is a whore.' Both men and women use this phrase to abuse a man

(116) زنِ کُس ده

zani kusdih: 'your wife is a cunt-giver': your wife is a whore. Both men and women use this phrase to abuse a man

# WORD FINDER & SPELLING CHECKER OR, SOME OF MY BEST FRIENDS ARE KNITTERS

(Reinhold Aman)

Word Finder™ is an excellent electronic thesaurus for the Macintosh computer. It contains of 220,000 synonyms for 15,000 key words. While checking some 'offensive' words, I found that the inclusion of such words is idiosyncratic. It contains such words as **asshole, prick, schmuck, shit, tit,** and **turd,** but neither **balls, broad** (female), **cock, cunt, dick, fart, fuck, piss** (yet **pissed, piss off,** and **pissed off** showed up as synonyms for *aggravate/d*), **pussy** (sexual), **putzs,** and **twat,** nor any racial, religious or ethnic slurs, as far as I could see.

However, the thesaurus contains four synonyms for the noun *homosexual*: **bisexual, gay, lesbian** and **queer.** Further, when I requested synonyms for *fairy*, the screen displayed **fag** (but not **faggot**), **pansy** and **sissy.**

In order to amuse myself – I am easily amused – I ran the preceding text through the spelling checker program built into Microsoft's *Word* (versions 3.02 and 4.0) word-processing application. The program was unable to suggest any alternative spellings for **fuck** and **schmuck,** but it did suggest the alternatives shown in parentheses for the following words in boldface: **asshole** (ashore, asphodel), **cunt** (cant, cent, chunk, churn, chute, chutney, count, cut, kung, sun, sung), **fag** (fig, fog, fug, phage; the 'word is already spelled correctly' in version 4.0), **fart** (Fahr, fair, far, fard, fat, fath, fear, fears, feast, fort), **putz** (but, butt, buzz, poult, pout, pouts, put, putt), **shit** (chit, shift, shipt, shirt, shot, shpt, shtg, shut, swift), **turd** (tour, toured, tours, thru, thrum, Thurs), and **twat** (dwt, thwart, thwarts, twit).

Continuing my amusement, I requested from the spelling checker more verbal nasties and got the following suggestions shown in parentheses for the words in boldface: **kike** (chide, chief, chile, chime, chine, chink, chinked, kiosk), **nigger** (knitter, nagger, Niger, Nigeria, niggler, nigglers, nudger, nudgers) and **spic** (skip, skips, spec, spice, spicy). The words **chink, kraut, Polack,** and **wop,** as well as **faggot, fairy, pansy, queer,** and **sissy** are 'already spelled correctly', according to version 4.0, thus no alternatives were suggested.

---

# ENGLISH

(Peter Kunzke)

I like your language
well enough.
It's well bred
of Anglo-Saxon stock
and well seasoned
with Latin and Greek.
It's the goddamned
fucked-up spellings
that annoy me.

# MORE TRADE NAMES OF AMERICAN CONDOMS

(Sir Maurice Sedley, *Bart*)

Rubber dubbing within the American condom manufacturing industry continues unabated. Twenty-three newly identified brand names fall into three of the previously identified general categories:

*Aggression* – 8; *Hedonism* – 12; *Morphology* or *Shape* – 3.

| AGGRESSION | HEDONISM |
|---|---|
| Banzai Bliss | Contact |
| Bareback | Diamond |
| Blazes | Double Play |
| Conquer | Fuji |
| Die-Hard | Glide |
| Round Up | Glow |
| Swashbuckler | Oriental Touch |
| Thunderfuck | Sensations |
| **MORPHOLOGY** or **SHAPE** | Slimscore |
| Decca-Stud | Super Score |
| Snugs | Waves |
| Wrinkle *Chapeau* Hard | Yield |

The augmented N of 75 names breaks down as follows into general categories:

| | | |
|---|---|---|
| Aggression: | N = 14 | 19% |
| Hedonism: | N = 41 | 55% |
| Morphology or Shape: | N = 9 | 12% |
| Neutrality: | N = 7 | 9% |
| Protection or Security: | N = 4 | 5% |

An analysis of the eight newly identified aggressive condom names indicates that seven of them imply a potentially violent assault on the feminine form, while one is openly defiant of femininity.

**Banzai Bliss:** The male as a fanatical, sabre-waving, shouting soldier charging across the field of Aphrodite to achieve victory over a feminine adversary. The name implies that the 'attack' will be delightfully successful.

**Bareback:** The male as a rough and ready horseman riding his feminine mount with a minimum of preliminaries.

**Blazes:** The male as an arsonist setting the female aflame with passion – the feminine form seen as a building to be torched by the fire of masculine passion.

**Conquer:** Woman as military objective to be subjugated.

**Die-Hard:** Male defiance in the face of certain loss of erection upon achieving orgasm upon the female body. Also, the name of a long-lasting battery.

**Round Up:** The male astride his 'horse of passion' going after his female 'heifer' to rope, bulldoze, tie and brand her.

**Swashbuckler:** The male as a sabre-waving, rope-swinging sea-dog boarding the female's 'vessel' afloat on the sea of passion.

**Thunderfuck:** The male as a noisy, Zeus-like divinity shooting his divine lightning into the female's yielding body. The picture on the package shows a Superman-like figure with a lightning bolt in one hand – both the name and the picture smack of grandiosity.

## HISTORICAL NOTE

Fallopius (1564) is credited with first describing the condom in European medical literature. The term *condom* first appears in England, in 1717, in Turner's treatise on syphilis, but to date, the etymology of the term remains unresolved.

# CHINESE VALUES AS DEPICTED IN MANDARIN TERMS OF ABUSE

(Shu-min Huang and D M Warren)

A study of verbal abuse in China faces several difficulties. The first is the tremendous language diversity. Besides the approximately fifty ethnic minorities – numbering around fifty million persons – the majority ethnic Chinese group, the Han, is also characterized by language diversity. There are nine major language groups among the majority Han Chinese, each of which is comprised of numerous dialects. In this study, we selected Mandarin, the official language of China, as our subject for analysis. Mandarin is the predominant indigenous language in north-central China; it is also used in official contexts and in school teaching throughout China. The terms of abuse in Mandarin may not be found in other Chinese languages, just as the other major languages of China may contain terms which have no equivalents in Mandarin.

The second difficulty faced in this study is the evasive quality of abusive terms used in Mandarin. Traditional Chinese culture strongly emphasizes literary achievements and appropriate and courteous behaviour. Using abusive terms is always discouraged among both children and adults. Given the long historical tradition in China, one finds that many abusive terms are euphemistic, wrapped in historical anecdotes and moral teachings. The user of certain abusive terms may know neither the exact meaning nor the origin of the terms. An analysis of the Mandarin abusive terms can, however, provide insights into the values of Chinese.

One value appears to be the relatively low status of women in traditional China. There are far more terms focusing on the

194

behaviour of women than on that of men. Women are considered potentially licentious, talkative, and untrustworthy. This reveals the male as a dominant value of traditional China. Another value reflected in the abuses is a negative nature of certain animals when associated with humans. The analogy between a person and such animals is definitely derogatory given the clear demarcation between humans and animals in traditional Chinese culture. Moving across this demarcation line is a certain means to degrade a person. Other Mandarin terms of abuse indicate a strong emphasis on proper behavioural conduct, particularly in terms of maintaining prescribed social relations. Conformity to existing hierarchical social relations – parent-child, superior-subordinate, emperor-common citizen, learnèd-illiterate – are underlying values found in many of the abusive terms. The deviation from such behavioural codes constitutes serious offences, the focus of many terms.

The three main categories of deviations attacked are physical, intellectual, social; within these groups they are categorized by provenance; and within these subgroups, alphabetically.

## PRONUNCIATION GUIDE

The romanization system used in this article follows the Pinyin system as it is used in current official Chinese literature. Basically, the **J** sounds as in 'jeer'; **q** as in '**cheer**'; **x** as in 'ship'; **z** as in 'zeal'; **zh** (sometimes also indicated as ẑ) is a voiced *z* with the tip of the tongue rolled back to the temple area; no such sound in English; **c** as in 'rats' or 'train'; **ch** (same as ĉ) is a voiced *c*, with the tip of the tongue to the temple area; no equivalent sound in English; **s** as in 'sand'; **sh** (same as ŝ) is a voiced *s*, with the tip of the tongue rolled back to the temple area; no equivalent sound in English; **ü** as in '**youth**' or in German *über*. Tones: 'rising; 'falling; ˇ falling, then rising.

# MANDARIN TERMS OF ABUSE

## I Insults Attacking Physical Deviations and Shortcomings

### A. Body (size, shape, function)

#### 1. Human Provenance

(1) 矮子

ăi-ze: 'short junior': a dwarf; a short man. *Ze* is a diminutive meaning 'minor, guy, fellow'. Mostly referring to males

(2) 癩子

lài-ze: 'blotty person': one who has stain-like spots on the skin resembling cankers or lesions; a blotty fellow

(3) 秃子

tū-ze: 'bald junior': as man who has no hair due to a physiological problem; 'baldy'

#### 2. Animal Provenance

(4) 独眼竜

dú-yěn-lún: 'one-eyed dragon': a man who has lost an eye

(5) 秃驴

tū-l ü: 'bald donkey': a bald man who resembles a donkey; also, a monk

#### 3. Plant Provenance

(6) 残花败柳

cán-hūa bài-lĭu: 'faded flowers and withered willows': a fallen woman; a woman beyond her prime age of beauty

#### 4. Objects Provenance

(7) 开天窗

kāi tīen-chūang: 'open-sky window': a person who has syphilis which has resulted in muscle deterioration or scarring on the forehead

## 5. Body Parts Provenance

(8) 笨手笨脚

bèn-shǒu bèn-jiǎo: 'clumsy hand and clumsy leg': a person who lacks adroitness

(9) 罗汉腿

ló-hàn tuěi: 'legs like Arhan': a man who has bandy legs. Arhan was one of Buddha's 500 disciples; they often squatted on the ground while crossing their legs, resulting in bandied legs

(10a) 他妈的

tā-mā-de:

(10b) 妈的尼

mā-de-bī: 'his mother's . . . ', 'mother's cunt': common terms expressing disapproval or disappointment; vulgar but not insulting terms; equivalent to 'damn it!' in English

### B. Cleanliness

#### 1. Human Provenance

(11) 臭娘子

còu-biǎo-ze: 'stinky whore': an insult to a woman who is not actually a whore

#### 2. Objects Provenance

(12) 邋遢

lā-tā: 'slovenly disgusting': a person who appears dirty in dress or physical appearance

#### 3. Body Parts Provenance

(13) 臭鸡巴

còu jī bā: 'stinky vulva': an insult to a woman

# II Insults Attacking Intellectual and Mental Deviations and Shortcomings

#### 1. Human Provenance

(14) 傻子

shǎ-ze: 'stupid junior': a foolish, gullible man

(15) 幼稚

yòu-zè: 'young child': an immature, unsophisticated person; an ignoramus

## 2. Animal Provenance

(16) 井底之蛙

jǐng-dǐzē wā: 'well-bottom frog': a person who has narrow perceptions or views on anything, like a frog who sits at the bottom of a well; an ignorant and arrogant person

(17) 驴旦

lú-dàn: 'donkey's balls': a person as stupid as a donkey. *Dàn* literally means 'eggs'; cf. German vulgar *Eier* 'balls'

(18) 无头苍蝇

wú-tóu chāng-yíng: 'headless fly': a mindless person

## 3. Body Parts Provenance

(19) 笨旦

bèn dàn: 'foolish balls': a born fool; an idiot. *See* No. 17.

(20) 六神无主

lìu-shéng wú-zhǔ: 'six souls without a master': an absent-minded person; a mindless person. All living Chinese are considered to have six different souls; a deceased Chinese is considered to have seven spirits

(21) 失魂落魄

shē-húen lò-pò: 'lost soul and discarded spirit': a mindless person

(22) 心理变态

xīn-lǐ bièn-tài: 'distorted mind': a psychotic person

## 4. Characteristics Provenance

(23) 结结巴巴

jié-jié bā-bā: 'stammering': a tongue-tied person; an inarticulate person. Two types of stammering are distinguished in Mandarin

(24) 无知

wú zhē: 'no knowledge'; 'void of knowledge': an ignorant person who has neither formal education nor common-sense knowledge

### 5. Plant Provenance

(25a) 傻瓜
shǎ-gūa:

(25b) 呆瓜
dāi-gūa: 'stupid melon': a foolish or gullible person

## III Insults Attacking Individual and Social Deviations and Shortcomings

### A. Character and Personality

#### 1. Human Provenance

(26) 利害
lì-hài: 'sharp and damaging': a shrewd person

(27) 意气用事
ì-qì iòng-shè: 'emotion dominates events': a person who loses control over himself or herself

#### 2. Animal Provenance

(28) 雌老虎
cē-lǎo-hǔ: 'old female tiger': a derogatory term for a woman who is dominant and short-tempered

#### 3. Body Parts Provenance

(29) 狠心
hěn-xīn: 'cruel heart': a cruel person

#### 4. Characteristics Provenance

(30) 残忍
cán-rěn: 'brutal patience': a person who inflicts extraordinary sufferings on others and who enjoys witnessing other persons' sufferings

(31) 老顽固
lǎo wán-kù: 'old stubborn': a stubborn old man

(32) 迷信
mí-xìn: 'confused belief': a superstitious person

(33) 虛榮

    **xü-rúng**: 'unreal glory': a vain person

    B. Personal Conduct and Behavioural Patterns

        *1. Human Provenance*

(34) 敗家精

    **bài-jīa jīng**: 'failing family demon': a person who wastes the family fortune, resulting in the downfall of the family

(35) 敗家子

    **bài-jīa zě**: 'failing family junior': a man who wastes the family fortune, resulting in the downfall of the family

(36) 村夫愚妇

    **chūn-fū yü-fù**: 'village husband and stupid wife': ignorant peasants

(37) 二毛子

    **èr máo-ze**: 'second-class hairy people': Chinese Christians who use their religious prestige to oppress other Chinese. The Chinese converts are called 'second-class hairy people' because the missionaries, who are mainly Westerners, are called **da máo-ze**, 'the big hairy people'.

(38) 漢奸

    **hàn-jīen**: 'Han Chinese traitor': a Chinese who collaborates with a foreign war-time enemy

(39) 奸夫淫妇

    **jīen-fū yín-fù**: 'adulterous man and licentious woman': male and female adulterers

(40) 奸商

    **jīen-shāng**: 'treacherous merchants': dishonest businessmen. Traditional Chinese social values placed merchants at the bottom of the four major social categories of intellectuals, farmers, craftsmen, and merchants. Businessmen are regarded as always being greedy, manipulative and dishonest

(41) 奸细

    **jīen-xì**: 'adulterous petty person': a spy or traitor who works for any opposing power

(42) 老不死

    **lăo-bù-sě**: 'old, but not yet dead': a useless old man

(43) 乞丐

    **qǐ-gài**: 'beggar': a poor person who lives by begging

(44) 人尽可夫

    **rén jìn kě:-fū**: 'every man can be the husband': a lascivious woman who takes any man as a lover or husband

(45) 三姑六婆

    **sān-gū liù-pó**: 'three aunts and six grandmothers': women indulging in gossip

(46) 守财奴

    **shǒu-cái-nú**: 'Property-guarding slave': a stingy rich man who guards his property so relentlessly that he himself looks like a slave

(47) 贪官污吏

    **tān-gūan wū-lì**: 'greedy officials and corrupted administrators': government officials who are objectionable to the public. This term has been popular during the revolutionary period

(48) 亡国奴

    **wáng-gúo nú**: 'lost country slave': a person whose own country has been conquered by an enemy, the person having become a slave of the conquering power

(49) 亡命之徒

    **wáng-mìn zē-tú**: 'lost life people': an outlaw or desperado; a villain who does not care about his or her own life

(50) 相公

    **xiàng-gūng**: 'young gentleman': a catamite; a boy kept for a pederastic purposes

(51) 乡愿

    **xīang-yuèn**: 'an old country man': a man who tries to please everyone; a 'yes man'

(52) 小什种

    **xiǎo-zá-zǔng**: 'little bastard': a person whose mother is sexually loose; hence one is not certain about his or her real father

(53) 洋奴买办

**yáng-nú mǎi-bàn:** 'foreign slave and agent': commercial agents for foreign companies; collaborators of a foreign country who work only for material gains

(54) 要死不活

**yào-sě bù-húo:** 'looks dying, not alive': a person who has no strength or tenacity

### 2. *Animal Provenance*

(55) 吹牛

**chuēi-níu:** 'blowing up the bull': a braggart who blows up a dead bull's hide to make it look bigger

(56) 狗娘养的

**gō-níang yǎng-de:** 'raised by a dog's mother': an insult to a person which implies that his/her mother is a dog. Equivalent to 'son of a bitch' in English

(57) 龟儿子

**guēi ér-ze:** 'turtle's son': an insult to a man which implies that his mother was loose enough to have been impregnated by a turtle

(58) 龟公

**guēi-gōng:** 'male turtle': a pimp

(59) 龟孙子

**guēi sūn-ze:** 'turtle's grandson': an insult to a man which implies that his grandmother was sexually loose enough to have been impregnated by a turtle

(60) 混旦

**huèn-dàn:** 'scoundrel's balls': a rowdy blackguard. *See* No. 17

(61) 癞蛤蟆

**lài-há-ma:** 'a blotty toad': a man who doesn't realize the extent of his own ugly appearance; one who chases after pretty girls despite an ugly appearance; a man who lacks self-estimation

(62) 色鬼

**shè-kuěi:** 'lustful ghost': a person, especially a man, who engages in continuous sexual adventures

(63) 色狼

**shè-láng:** 'lustful wolf': a person, especially a man, who engages in continuous sexual adventures

(64) 色魔

**shè-mó:** 'lustful demon': a person, especially a man, who engages in continuous sexual adventures

(65) 鼠辈

**sǔ-bèi:** 'rat's companions': thieves

(66) 兔崽子

**tù-sǎi-ze:** 'rabbit's illegitimate son': a male homosexual

(67) 忘八旦

**wáng-bā dàn:** 'forgotten eight virtues' balls': a man who forgets about the eight cardinal virtues of life (filial piety, brotherly submission, loyalty, sincerity, propriety, righteousness, modesty and a sense of shame); a valueless human being (17)

(68) 走狗

**zhǒu-gǒu:** 'running dog': a person who is willingly manipulated by others behind the scenes; collaborators with a foreign power, especially during the war

(69) 豬猡

**zhū-ló:** 'pig': a man who acts or eats like a pig; a dirty and greedy person

### 3. Objects Provenance

(70) 党棍

**dǎng-gùn:** 'party stick': a party loyalist who lives by promoting party propaganda. The term 'stick' refers to inflexibility, something solid and without its own mind

(71) 地痞

**dì-pí:** 'rough earth': a rascal; a person without a stable job

(72) 教棍

**jiào-gùn:** 'religious stick': a devout religious follower who lives by selling his or her beliefs

(73) 尖酸刻薄

jīen-shuān kè-bó: 'sharp acid cuts thin': a sarcastic person; a person whose sharp tongue can ridicule anything at any moment

(74) 流氓

líu-máng: 'a drifter': a man with no stable occupation

(75) 轻浮

qīng-fú: 'light and floating': a weightless person who acts restlessly

(76) 书呆子

shū-dāi-ze: 'book idiot': a bookworm

(77) 水性扬花

suěi-xìn yáng-hūa: 'water that flows up flowers': a sexually loose woman who indulges in seducing men; an unstable, fickle woman

(78) 无赖

wú-lài: 'no dependency': a person with no stable job or occupation

(79) 下流

xià-liú: 'lower stream': a lower-class man who takes advantage of others, especially of women. The term *liú* literally means river or stream, but refers to social class here

(80) 邪门外道

xié-mén wài-dàu: 'lopsided/oblique door and illegitimate path': one who does not follow correct or legitimate ways in conducting one's affairs

(81) 烟枪

yēn-qīang: 'smoking gun': a heavy user of tobacco

(82) 朝秦暮楚

zāu-qíng mù-chǔ: 'morning Qing kingdom, evening Chu kingdom': a capricious person. This is taken from an ancient Chinese story of about the third century BC; a man who pledged his loyalty to the Qing kingdom in the morning and then switched to Chu, the opposing kingdom, in the evening

## 4. Body Parts Provenance

### A. Human

(83) 财迷心窍

**cái-mí xīn-qiào:** 'wealth blocks the heart aperture': a person who is so obsessed by greed that he or she loses his or her mind

(84) 操你妈的

**càu-nǐ-mā-dè:** 'fuck your mother's . . .': an insult to a person by implying the speaker having sexual intercourse with the person's mother. In some cases, the word *bī* ('cunt') is added to it to make a complete sentence

(85) 長舌妇

**cháng-shé fù:** 'long-tongued woman': a talkative woman who passes on gossip

(86) 触霉头

**chù-méi-tóu:** 'gore/bump into the mildewed head': an act which brings bad luck to the receiving party

(87) 拉皮条

**lā-pí-tiáo:** 'pulling on strips of skin/leather thongs': a pimp; one who lives by matching up adulterous men with women

(88) 毛手毛脚

**máo-shǒu máo-jiǎu:** 'hairy hands and hairy legs': a man who intentionally touches a woman while making sexual advances

(89) 没种

**méi-zhǔng:** 'lack of seeds/balls': a gutless coward; a man without the seeds to produce offspring. *Zhǔng* 'seed, semen; testes'

(90) 皮厚

**pí-hòu:** 'thick skin': a bold, audacious person

(91) 软骨头

**ruǎn gǔ-táu:** 'soft boned': a pimp; a spineless person who lives off women

(92) 乳臭未干
rǔ-còu wèi-gān: 'milk stink not dry': an immature person;
a man who hasn't yet grown up

(93) 三隻手
sān zē shǒu: 'three-handed': a pickpocket or thief

(94) 死皮癞脸
sě-pí lài-liěn: 'dead skin and blotchy face': a shameless
person who insists on making excessive demands on
others. This is usually used by women to refer to a man
who insists on having sexual adventures even after continuous rebuttals by the woman

(95) 贪咀
tān-zuěi: 'greedy mouth': a gluttonous person

(96) 想入非非
xiǎng-rè fēi-fēi: 'imagining to enter a hairy area': a person
who indulges in sexual fantasies. *Xiǎng* 'imagining, long-
ing for, wishing to, thinking of'. The term for 'hairy'
originally referred to vulva

(97) 小白脸
xiǎo bái-liěn: 'small, light-skinned face': a gigolo; a male
who lives off women through his good looks. The term
'light-skinned' is a reference to persons of the upper class
who don't get tanned skins as they don't work outdoors

(98) 小气
xiǎo-qì: 'petty spirited': a petty-minded, mean person

(99) 小偷
xiǎo-tōu: 'petty thief': a pickpocket or thief

(100) 心狠手辣
xīn-hěng shǒu-là: 'cruel mind and hot hands': a cruel
person who enjoys inflicting physical injuries upon others

(101) 油咀滑舌
yīo-zuěi húa-shé: 'oily mouth and slippery tongue': a glib
person who manipulates words in such a way that he or
she turns a serious conversation into a farce

(102) 贼头贼脑
zéi-tóu zéi-nǎu: 'thief's head and thief's brain': a person

who behaves like a thief by sneaking behind other persons
or by peeping at the activities of others

(103) 叫 饞

zuěi-cán: 'craving mouth': a gluttonous person

## B. Animal

(104) 狗屁

gǒu-pì: 'dog's fart': a worthless person; worthless words
or opinions

(105) 狗腿子

gǒu tuěi-ze: 'dog's legs': one who runs errands for villains.
It used to refer to collaborators of the Japanese during
World War II

(106) 狼心狗肺

lán-xīn gǒu-fèi: 'wolf's heart and dog's liver': a heartless,
cruel person

(107) 马屁精

mǎ-pì-jīn: 'horse fart spirit': a fawning flatterer

(108) 拍马屁

pāi mǎ-pì: 'petting a horse's buttock': a fawning flatterer

(109) 蛇蠍心腸

shé-xiè xīn-cháng: 'snake's and scorpion's heart and intestines':
a cruel heartless person, often referring to women

(110) 熊心豹胆

xíung-xīng bào-dǎn: 'bear's heart and leopard's gall': a
bold, audacious person

## 5. Abstract Provenance

(111) 尅夫命

kē-fū mìn: 'against the husband's fate': a woman who
brings bad fortune to her husband

(112) 喪尽天良

sàng jìn tīen-líang: 'completely lost heavenly conscience':
a person who has lost all of his or her conscience

(113) 忘恩负义

wàng-ēn fù-yì: 'forgotten favours, betrayed justice': a
person who betrays friends who have done favours for
him or her

(114)无法无天

**wú-fǎ wú-tīen:** 'no law, no heaven': a person who has no respect for any existing rules or laws

(115)愚孝

**yú-xiào:** 'foolish filial piety': a person who is foolishly loyal to undeserving parents or ancestors

(116)愚忠,

**yú-zhūng:** 'foolish loyalty': a person who is foolishly loyal to an undeserving superior or an emperor

(117)朝三暮四

**zāu-sān mù-sè:** 'morning three, dusk four': a person who is not consistent. This is taken from an ancient Chinese story dating to the third century BC in which a man promised his monkeys three chestnuts in the morning and four in the evening. The monkeys objected, so he changed to four in the morning and three in the evening, and then they accepted. It is used to illustrate how to swindle one through clever tricks

### 6. *Activity Provenance*

(118)搬弄是非

**bān-lòn shè-fēi:** 'manipulating the truth and falsehoods': a person who enjoys spreading gossip in order to create disputes

(119)班门弄斧

**bān-mén lùn-fǔ:** 'handling/playing with an axe in front of the master craftsman Ban's front door gate': an ignorant braggart. This is taken from a historical story which originated around the third or fourth century BC in which an ignorant person was bragging about how well he could handle his craftsman's tools, not knowing that he was bragging in front of the house of Mr Ban, a real master craftsman

(120)吃软饭

**chē rǔan-fàn:** 'eating soft rice': a pimp; a man who depends upon women for a living

(121)吹毛求疵

**chuēi-máo qíu-cě:** 'blowing hair to find a flaw': a person who searches for trifling defects, as a person who looks

for flaws in a piece of beautiful fur by blowing up the fur
during the search

(122) 千人骑，万人压

**cīen-rén qí, wàn-rén īa:** 'thousands ride, ten thousands
mount': a whore who is mounted by thousands of men
during her life

(123) 反覆无常

**fǎn-fù wú-cháng:** 'repeatedly turns around without
consistence': a person who changes his or her mind con-
tinuously; a disloyal subordinate who betrays the master

(124) 盲从

**máng-chóng:** 'blindly following': a person who has no
personal opinion or idea but rather blindly follows others

(125) 数典忘祖

**shù-diěn wàng-zhǔ:** 'thumbing through ancient scripts
and forgetting the ancestors': a traitor; a person who
betrays his or her ancestors despite a proper training

(126) 贪小

**tān-xiǎo:** 'craving for small things': a greedy person who
seeks to obtain petty advantages over other people

(127) 挑拨是非

**tiǎu-pūo shè-fēi:** 'stirring up truth with falsehoods': a
person who spreads gossip in order to provoke conflict

(128) 投机取巧

**tóu-jī qǔ-qiǎo:** 'jump into opportunity for advantages': an
opportunist

## 7. Characteristics Provenance

(129) 霸道

**bà-dàu:** 'the way of might': an unreasonable person who
brushes his or her way over other person's rights, in
contrast to 'the way of right'

(130) 不要脸

**bú yào liěn:** 'doesn't care about losing face': a shameless
person who doesn't care about losing face through misconduct

(131) 奸诈

**jīen-zà:** 'wickedly deceptive': a person who is artfully
fraudulent

(132)斤斤计较

**jīn-jīn jì-jiǎo:** 'catty by catty/one by one counting': a stingy person who argues with other people over trifling matters. The 'catty' is a small weight unit equivalent to 1.33 lbs

(133) 烂货

**làn-huò:** 'rotten stuff': a licentious person, usually referring to women

(134)麻木不仁

**má-mù bù-rén:** 'numb and not kind': a person who has no sentiment or feelings towards other human beings

(135)没家教

**méi jīa-jiào:** 'without family teaching': a ruleless, disobedient person

(136) 娘娘腔

**niáng-niáng qiang:** 'feminine vocal tones': a man who speaks and acts like a woman; an effeminate man

(137)骗子

**pièn-ze:** 'cheater': a quack; a charlatan

(138) 骚货

**shāu-huò:** 'rank-smelling stuff': a woman who seeks to attract the attention of men

(139) 十恶不赦

**shé-è bú shè:** 'ten crimes unredeemable': a person who has committed all ten unpardonable crimes (rebellion, conspiracy against a ruler, treason, patricide, murder or mutilation, sacrilege, unfilial behaviour, lack of harmony, insubordination, and incest); an unredeemable, guilt-ridden person

(140) 贪得无厌

**tān dé wú-yièn:** 'greed without tiring': a greedy person with insatiable needs

(141)忘本

**wàng běn:** 'forgotten origin': one who has forgotten his or her own ancestry

(142) 无能

**wú-néng:** 'without ability': a useless, impotent person

(143)喜新厌苗

**xǐ-xīn yèn-jìou:** 'love new, abhor old': a man who abandons his old wife for other women, particularly younger women

(144) 虚伪

**xū-wǎi:** 'pretentiously unreal': a person filled with vanity; a hypocrite

(145) 依老卖老

**yī-lǎo mài-lǎo:** 'depending on one's age to sell age': an old person who insists on the superiority of his or her opinion or views merely because of greater age

(146) 阴险

**yīn-xiěn:** 'surreptitious danger': a treacherous person who covers up his or her own emotion or opinion, but takes opportunities to damage other persons

(147) 阴阳怪气

**yīn-yáng guài-qì:** 'male-female confused essence': a man behaving like a woman; a person with an unpredictable personality

### 8. *Spirit Provenance*

(148) 恶魔

**è-mó:** 'malicious devil': one who commits a series of bad deeds

(149) 狐狸精

**hú-lí-jing:** 'female fox's/vixen's spirit': a woman who has special talent in seducing men

(150) 酒鬼

**jiǒu-guěi:** 'liquor ghost': an alcoholic or drunkard. The 'ghost' in this instance is malicious

(151) 穷光旦

**quóng gūang-dàn:** 'poor as a bald egg': a poor person

(152) 穷鬼

**quóng-guěi:** 'poor ghost': a poor person

(153) 无药可救

**wú-yiào kě-jiù:** 'no medicine can save': a hopeless person; a hopelessly ill, dying person

(154) 妖精

**yiāo-jīng:** 'female demon's spirit': a woman who has special talent in seducing men.

# LIST OF CONTRIBUTORS

**Reinhold Aman,** PhD, Medieval Literatures and Germanic Philology

**Giuliano Averna,** Italian Poet

**Fiach Ó Broin,** Irish Writer

**Bob Burton Brown,** PhD, Professor of Education

**Richard Christopher,** PhD, Professor of English

**Martha Cornog,** MA, Bibliographer and Sex Researcher

**Sterling Eisiminger,** PhD, Professor of English

**Tim Healey,** MD, British Radiologist and Surgeon

**L Herrera,** PhD, Professor of French

**Shu-min Huang,** PhD, Professor of Anthropology and Chinese

**Zack Isović,** MA, Teacher and Slavic Dancer

**David Lindsey,** MD, Professor and Surgeon

**Jess Nierenberg,** MA, Folklorist and Translator

**Soraya Noland,** PhD, Professor of Anthropology and Persian

**Joel Oppenheimer,** Poet and Columnist

**Elias Petropoulos,** Greek Folklorist and Writer

**Robert St Vincent Phillippe,** PhD, Professor of French

**Joseph Salemi,** PhD, Professor of English and Classics

**Clifford J Scheiner,** MD, Surgeon and Rare Books Dealer

**Rudolf Schmid,** PhD, Professor of Biology

**Sir Maurice Sedley,** Baronet, EdD

**Andrew R Sisson,** PhD, Professor of French

**John Solt,** PhD, Professor of Japanese

**Mario E Teruggi,** PhD, Professor of Geology and Linguist

**Dennis Michael Warren,** PhD, Professor of Anthropology and African Languages